IF LIFE IS A BALANCING ACT, WHY AM I SO DARN CLUMSY?

Progressing Beyond Professional Success to Personal Happiness

by

Dick Biggs

Chattahoochee Publishers
420 Market Place, Suite 108
Roswell, Georgia 30075
(404) 998-5452

First printing 1993

ISBN 0-9635977-6-0

LCCN 93-70774

Design, typesetting, and printing services provided by About Books, Inc., 425 Cedar Street, Buena Vista, CO 81211, 800-548-1876.

ATTENTION CORPORATIONS, ASSOCIATIONS, COLLEGES, AND ORGANIZATIONS: Quantity discounts are available on bulk purchases of this book for educational purposes or fund raising. Special books or book excerpts can also be created to fit specific needs. For information, please contact Chattahoochee Publishers, 420 Market Place, Suite 108, Roswell, Georgia 30075 or call (404) 998-5452.

Dedication

This book is a tribute to three special people.

First, I salute my parents—Daniel K. Biggs of St. Petersburg, Florida and Thelma P. (Hall) Askew of Elberton, Georgia—for instilling in me the Christian values that shaped my formative years.

Second, I owe an enormous debt of gratitude to my wife. Judy is responsible for reviving my dormant spiritual life after a long hiatus. She also inspired and encouraged me to finish this book when I quit on several occasions.

To Dad, Mom and Judy . . . I love you!

Acknowledgments

As a reader, I wouldn't be surprised if you overlooked this section. However, it would be impossible for this author to omit these pages. While my name may appear on the front of this book, it's truly the collective efforts of many people. Allow me to acknowledge the names of those who—directly and indirectly—helped turn this massive project into a reality.

Besides the influence of my parents and wife cited on the dedication page, I'm grateful for the support of the rest of my family. To Rebecca and Tara Stvan, my stepdaughters . . . Beryl, Carol and Amy Johnson, brother-in-law, sister and adorable niece . . . Larry, Sharon and Christopher O'Bryant, brother-in-law, sister and talented nephew . . . Bob Biggs, my only brother . . . and all the other relatives too numerous to name.

Special thanks to Dr. Gene Griessman, Dr. Ken Boa and Beth Leahy. Gene not only read the manuscript and offered invaluable advice, but he also challenged me to realize my goal of publishing a book. Ken graciously read the manuscript, suggested some important changes and wrote the foreword. And Beth, a former English teacher, neighbor and friend, provided some much needed editing and insight. She did so while running a business with husband Mike, raising two young daughters and undergoing a family tragedy.

I'm grateful to Linda Tamburrino, a high school classmate and owner of LMT Computer Service, Inc., for processing the manuscript into a computer . . . and to C. Richard Weylman, a close friend and nationally-acclaimed speaker, for talking me into changing my original, academic title to the more upbeat one I wrote after much soulsearching.

Naturally, I'm indebted to the many friends who allowed me to use their stories throughout this book. I also appreciate my many friends at Roswell United Methodist Church, including the Bereans Sunday school class . . . to the members of the Chattahoochee Road Runners, Atlanta Track Club, Georgia Speakers Association, National Speakers Association and National Vehicle Leasing Association—you know who you are. And to my classmates and teachers at East Atlanta High School . . . my former Marine buddies Bob Hollenbaugh, Pete Jaynes, Bob Lenneman, Tony Ranallo, Al Rupich, Ken Tapp and J. D. Taylor . . . and dear friends Bob and Lynda Connor, Frank and Linda Crane, Ron and Sharon Creasy, Ken and Linda Futch and Richard and Jackie Weylman.

Finally, my hat is off to Tom and Marilyn Ross and their friendly, professional staff at About Books, Inc. in Buena Vista, Colorado for shepherding the intricate task of book publishing and marketing.

Foreword

Men lust, but they know not what for;
They wander, and lose track of the goal;
They fight and compete, but they forget the prize;
They spread seed, but spurn the seasons of growth;
They chase power and glory, but miss the meaning of
*   life.*

— *George Gilder*

■ ■ ■

Few people would embark on a journey without knowing their destination and making the necessary plans to reach it. But when it comes to the most important journey of all—our life's journey—the majority of us fail to ask the tough question, What do I want my life to add up to, and why? When I reach the end of my years and look over my shoulder at the past, what will it take for me to say I led a satisfied life? If we're not careful, we may slip into the trap of straining at the gnats of our short-term goals while swallowing the camel of our life's purpose.

My friend Max Anders tells the story of a mother who one night fixed a special meal for her family: turkey with mashed potatoes and gravy, corn, green beans, cranberry sauce and apple pie. It was everyone's favorite meal, especially when it came at a time other than Thanksgiving. The aroma filled the house, and as the children came in from playing, they could hardly wait for dinner to begin. The last child appeared only a few minutes before dinner time and sat through the meal without eating, even though he especially loved those foods. Why? Because he had filled up on peanut butter at a friend's house. In settling for something good, he had lost his appetite for the best.

The good can become the enemy of the best when we settle for toys and trinkets and miss out on the things that will really last. "It is not a tragedy to die for something you believe in, but it is a tragedy to find at the end of your life that what you believed in betrayed you." That statement, attributed to Joan of Arc, captures the essence of our ongoing struggle between the claims of a cultural and superficial view of success and those of a lasting view of success. It is a question of values—the greatest good in life is to treat things according to their true value. Wisdom urges us to give our lives in exchange for the things that are important. It has been observed that no one on his or her death bed ever regretted not having spent more time at the office. The regrets of life have to do with incomplete relationships, because at the end of the day, relationships are what life is really about.

Consider the quest for status: know it all, show it all, owe it all. People buy things they don't need with money they don't have to impress people they don't even like! When this happens, the order of the day is "blowing and going, plotting and planning, ducking and diving." Without a clear sense of purpose, identity, conviction, and hope, we become human doings rather than human beings.

Success is the progressive realization of a worthwhile dream or goal. It is a growth process, not merely a product; it is a progression, not a static state. When doing is more fundamental to us than being, life gets so filled with the if onlys of the future that today becomes an inconvenient obstacle in the path of reaching tomorrow. And yet today is all we have. Life is filled with todays, because living is so daily. Walker Percy observed that to live in the past and the future is easy. To live in the present is like threading a needle.

On Arturo Toscanini's 80th birthday, someone asked his son, Walter, what his father ranked as his most important achievement. The son replied, "For him there can be no such thing. Whatever he happens to be doing at the moment is the biggest thing in his life—whether it is conducting a symphony or peeling an orange."

The book you now hold is filled with wisdom and insights on what it takes to enjoy your life's journey. I know Dick Biggs well enough to assure you that he is not writing out of theory or secondhand experience. He has hammered out these principles on the anvil of his own successes and failures, and what you read is what he is. When you read chapters about integrity, honesty, faith, purpose, applied knowledge, vision, resourcefulness, wisdom, discipline, dependability, perseverance, spiritual influence and dignity, Dick knows whereof he speaks.

Dr. Kenneth Boa
Eastern Divisional Director
Search Ministries, Inc.
Atlanta, Georgia

Table of Contents

Part I
"To Be"

Part II
"To Think"

Part III
"To Do"

Part IV
"To Have"

Introduction

"Living is a balancing act in which we measure the importance of every experience by where it fits between right and wrong, sadness and happiness, failure and success."

— *Elmo Ellis*
Happiness Is Worth The Effort

■ ■ ■

I once heard a speaker remark, "I've never known any successful business person who had balance in their life." Although I didn't realize it at the time, those words would become my motivation for writing this book. It occurred to me that terms such as balance of nature, balance of power, balance of trade and corporate balance statements are quite common. Shouldn't a balanced lifestyle be normal, too?

Alas, the world is full of "successful" professionals craving for personal happiness. Sounds contradictory, doesn't it? After all, doesn't enormous business success ensure abundant personal happiness? Unquestionably, a part of personal happiness is career achievement. Yet, without a measure of balance, the scales of life become top heavy. Burn out is usually the end result. Burned out people lack balance, which is essential for professional success AND personal happiness.

An IBM advertisement once put it this way: "The newest national pastime—trying to strike a balance between the work you do and the life you lead." By no means am I suggesting such harmony is necessarily a 50-50 split between one's career and personal life or that precise balance is always possible each day. The idea is to strive for a reasonable measure of long-term balance just as you'd strive for a reasonable measure of diversity over the years with your financial investments. In *The Paradox Of Success*, John R. O'Neil refers to these people as "long-distance winners" who "have learned how to keep their pursuit of excellence in balance with their inner well-being."

Clearly, there is a major difference between professional success and personal happiness. Understanding this difference is the key to living a balanced life. Typically, professional success is measured externally by comparisons to tangibles such as an employer, job title, income, homes, automobiles, clothing, jewelry, appearance, friends, memberships in various organizations and other material possessions.

On the other hand, personal happiness is measured intangibly from within and is focused on the spiritual side of life. Tangibly, a person may be incredibly successful due to a prosperous career. Still, no amount of intelligence, wealth, power or status can guarantee happiness. Why? Because real happiness is a feeling that can only be enjoyed if we're true to ourselves and others; and provided we direct these values of integrity and honesty toward a meaningful purpose based on serving others and honoring God in all we think, say and do.

While this book is not a religious text, my religious beliefs are very much a part of this work. We all have a philosophy of life and mine is Christian-based. That's who I am and what I believe. I make no apology for expressing my value system even though it might differ from yours. I only ask that you read what I have to say about balanced living with an open mind. I believe you'll discover nuggets of truth no matter what your philosophy of life might be.

Surely, most people yearn for a more balanced lifestyle, but how do we become more balanced? I believe the answers can be found in the understanding of four powerful forces which, if aligned properly, will enable us to cultivate the difficult but doable task of balancing professional success and personal happiness.

Those four forces are:

1. **To Be**—This is the spiritual force. It centers on a person's character and the development of a worthwhile purpose in life.

2. **To Think**—This is the mental force. It concentrates on the pursuit of knowledge and a person's goals, attitude, desire, motivation and many other qualities.

3. **To Do**—This is the physical force. It deals with the application of knowledge and getting things done efficiently and effectively.

4. **To Have**—This is the emotional force. It dwells on the enjoyment of life's true treasures.

I believe most people struggle with the issue of balanced living because they have these forces in the wrong order:

Have → Think → Do → Be = Unbalanced Lifestyle

Be → Think → Do → Have = Balanced Lifestyle

For example, people with an unbalanced lifestyle are often consumed with *having* material possessions. Next, they *think* about how these possessions will be acquired. Third, they attempt to *do* whatever is necessary to achieve these goals. Finally, as a rule, little or no emphasis is placed upon *being* people of sound character and meaningful purpose.

By contrast, people with a more balanced lifestyle arrange these forces in a different order. First, they try to *be* people of sound character and meaningful purpose. With such a spiritual foundation, they *think* differently and *do* things more dutifully. Lastly, they *have* special joys that no amount of money can buy, that no amount of professional success can match.

Just as a baby is clumsy while learning to walk, we're awkward when it comes to balancing our lives. An infant practices walking until it becomes second nature. No matter how many times a child falls, it keeps trying until walking becomes as normal as breathing. We, too, must understand the delicate alignment of the four forces of balanced living if we're to reap a bountiful harvest of professional success and personal happiness. No matter how many times we may stumble in our quest for a more stable lifestyle, we must believe our efforts will be richly rewarded.

Is your life out of balance? Are you successful at work, but lacking satisfaction in other areas of your life? Are you happy with your personal life, but struggling with your business career? Are both sides of your life in the pits? Or, would you simply like to improve the balanced lifestyle you already have? If you answered yes to any of these questions, read on.

You hold in your hands a small, simple book containing 100 essays to help you discover a more balanced lifestyle. An essay, according to Webster's, is nothing more than "a short literary composition dealing with a single subject, usually from a personal point of view and without attempting completeness." My wish is that these essays, based on the experience of a 47-year-old business owner and family man, will help you find optimal professional success and personal happiness. Could you ask for any more?

Remember, your life hangs in the balance!

PART I

"TO BE"

The Spiritual Force

"Life is not a having and a getting, but a being and a becoming."

— *Matthew Arnold*

1

The Value of Values

"(Values) must be taught in the home, in religious training, in the Boy Scouts, in Little League, in the media. And most critically, as a guarantee that everyone be exposed to them, they must be taught in the schools."

— *James A. Michener*

■　■　■

Essentially, values are taught in three critical areas of society—in the home, in the community and in religious training. If the training isn't done properly in the early years, more selfish and worldly value systems may take root. The values we learn in childhood—good or bad—are often the ones that guide us in adulthood.

Obviously, the home should be the bedrock for learning values. Unfortunately, this isn't always possible due to the fragmentation of families. Another way to instill values is through religious training, but what happens if children aren't exposed to theological teachings? Without proper values instruction in the home or religious training, that leaves the responsibility for teaching values to the community, with the school system at center stage.

In *The Day America Told The Truth*, authors James Patterson and Peter Kim stated: "The overwhelming majority of Americans (81 percent) want schools to teach morals to our children. What values (which means *whose* values) should be taught is one very real question. But most people are saying that it is better to learn values from a textbook than to not learn values at all."

While our educators and parents argue about what or whose values to teach, here are **Ten Values of Value** for consideration:

- ▸ *Integrity*—Be true to yourself.

- ▸ *Honesty*—Be open and fair with others.

- ▸ *Discipline*—Develop good work habits.

- ▸ *Justice*—Do what is right. Speak up when something is wrong.

- ▸ *Responsibility*—Be thoughtful of others in exercising your many freedoms.

- ▸ *Accountability*—Be considerate of the property of others.

- ▸ *Compassion*—Love and serve others.

- ▸ *Peace*—Be a non-violent ambassador.

- ▸ *Respect*—Be obedient to those in authority.

- ▸ *Humility*—Be gracious in successes and in setbacks.

These simple but profound principles shouldn't encroach on anyone's religion; would reinforce what is being taught in the home or, in many cases, fill a void in a broken or unstable family; and could provide a wonderful opportunity for our school systems to groom more value-centered young people for college, military service, the business community and elsewhere.

2

Integrity

"When we examine life and consider it in the long run, the odds for a successful conclusion are greatly on the side of those who believe in personal integrity and who follow the instructions of the Bible."

— *Cliff C. Jones*
Winning Through Integrity

■ ■ ■

Integrity is different from honesty. Integrity is being true to yourself. Honesty is being true to others. Before a person can be honest with others, integrity is essential.

There is no substitute for integrity since it's the foundation upon which soundness of character is built. Without integrity, a person's life is nothing more than an exercise in deception. When there is no integrity, all else is suspect.

The word inteGRITy includes the word grit, which Webster's defines as a "firmness of mind or spirit . . . unyielding courage." It takes a great deal of grit or courage to be true to yourself, to stand up for what you believe. Is it worth the effort? Emphatically, yes!

Integrity breeds respect and respect leads to influence. The awesome power of influencing the lives of other people should be based upon truth. For, as St. Augustine said many centuries ago, "When regard for the truth has broken down or even slightly weakened, all things remain doubtful."

Unfortunately, speaking the truth in America is under attack by groups ranging from certain television networks and print media to lobbyists and liberal activists. Their catch phrase is political correctness—a clever way of concealing the truth lest someone be offended. Baloney! We make a mockery out of personal integrity when we allow the media or any other group to disguise the truth in the name of political correctness.

The ageless model of truth and integrity is the life of Jesus Christ. He delivered the classic moral code in His Sermon On The Mount (Matthew 5-7). Within that Biblical passage is a marvelous blueprint for high moral conduct. While no one can ever completely live up to the example set by Christ and espoused by Him in the Sermon On The Mount, it's imperative *to strive* to be as true to yourself as possible.

When a person lacks integrity, it sends a clear message to the people around them that this person can't be trusted or respected. Without trust and respect, there can be no meaningful, long-term relationships. Life can be very lonely and shallow.

Orison Marden, author of *Pushing To The Front*, was a man who believed integrity and character form the cornerstone in building and maintaining true success. To those who would scoff at integrity as a self-righteous approach to living, they'd be wise to heed the early 20th century advice of Marden: "Achievement of true integrity and well-rounded character is in itself success."

3

Integrity Versus Image

"Identity is who we are and identification is what other people think we are. Most people spend so much time on identification that there is little time for identity. If you'll spend more time on identity, the identification will take care of itself."

— *Bishop Ernest Fitzgerald, Ret.*
United Methodist Church

■ ■ ■

True identity—or who a person really is—must always be based upon integrity. Identification—or what other people think a person is—is one's projected image or reputation, which might not be one's true identity.

When I decided to leave journalism in 1970 to enter the sales profession, I did so with a great deal of apprehension. In fact, I almost didn't make the change. I was struggling with my image of salespeople as fast-talking, high-pressuring and misleading.

A friend gave me some sound advice I've never forgotten. He told me I'd sell exactly as the person I am. If I had integrity, my customers would know and appreciate it. He said every profession has its disreputable element, including the sales profession. "Be true to yourself, honest with others and everything else will take care of itself," my friend promised. He was right.

Since entering the sales profession 23 years ago, I've tried very hard to make sure my integrity and image are one and the same. Naturally, I've been acutely aware of the poor image of my industry. While I can't be responsible for the unethical or unprofessional behavior of any of my competitors, I can be a worthy role model.

One of the ways I try to make a difference is by conducting seminars within my industry. While my niche is automobile lease training, I also weave a strong theme of ethics and professionalism into all my sessions. In truth, many automobile dealership sales and management people want to do the right thing. Unfortunately, some of them work for owners who use obsolete, fast-track sales systems designed to abuse their customers.

I'm reminded of a young man who attended one of my seminars in Dallas. He had just been promoted from salesman to sales manager at an Arkansas dealership. He sat on the front row and seemed genuinely interested in my message of ethics and professionalism.

After the session, I was waiting in the hotel lobby for a taxi to the airport. This young man spotted me, asked if he could share a ride and split the fare. I agreed. When we reached the airport, the fare was $40. We each paid $20, but the young man asked the taxi driver for a $40 receipt. As he pocketed the inflated receipt, he winked and boasted, "I learned that trick from my general manager!"

As I reflected upon that incident, two questions came to mind. How many other "tricks" had his general manager taught him? As a new sales manager, would he be teaching these "tricks" to his salespeople? It also reminded me of Ron Willingham's classic definition of selling in *Integrity Selling*: "Selling isn't something you do *to* someone, it's something you do *for* and *with* someone."

4

Reputation Versus Money

"If you have to choose between a good reputation and great wealth, choose a good reputation."
— Proverbs 22:1 (GNV)

■ ■ ■

There's nothing wrong in having great wealth. The wrongdoing is in sacrificing one's reputation for great riches. We can become incredibly prosperous provided we do it honorably. In truth, wealth without integrity leads to the poor house.

There's no doubt money is important. It provides for a better standard of living and offers a certain degree of security. It builds our homes, schools, churches, hospitals and business communities. It is the incentive that makes free enterprise and democracy thrive in America.

Without money, third world nations struggle with the basics we take for granted in America. The lack of a free market economy, coupled with the evil forces of communism, finally brought the USSR to its knees as many of the Soviet republics declared their independence and turned to free enterprise.

Yes, money is important, but reputation is more important. Our prisons are full of dealers and bankers, gangsters and politicians, gamblers and religious leaders, bank robbers and stockbrokers, automobile thieves and business owners, arsonists and lawyers who overlooked the wisdom of Proverbs 22:1.

A good reputation is like folding a parachute. If the job is done right a thousand times, it's no big deal; but if the job is messed up just once, it's big news. A good reputation is something a person can *live* with. A bad reputation is something a person can *lose* with.

No matter how much money a person makes in a lifetime, at death these assets become someone else's property. A reputation, good or bad, goes with a person to the grave but is often long remembered by others. Ivan the Terrible had great wealth but how do we remember him? William Booth, The Salvation Army founder, never had financial riches but how do we remember him?

Jack Eckerd, the founder of the drugstore chain bearing his name, is a wonderful example of a man who amassed great wealth and maintained an impeccable reputation. He's donated millions of dollars to various charitable organizations. He's been involved in helping emotionally troubled children, college students, juvenile detention centers, prison industries and many other causes.

Lawyer Rex Farrior had this to say about Jack Eckerd in *Eckerd: Finding The Right Prescription*, ". . . when a man has money, if you want to judge him, find out two things: how he made it and what he does with it, and by those standards, Jack's 100 percent."

5

Honesty

"He was a good father, husband and an honest man."
— Tombstone of David W. Sparks
(March 28, 1863-May 4, 1940)
Cades Cove, Tennessee

■ ■ ■

How will your tombstone read? Will you be remembered as a person who valued integrity (being true to yourself) and honesty (being truthful with others) or will you be remembered as a person who deceived and lied their way to so-called success?

An honest person enjoys a freedom of mind, body and spirit no dishonest person can ever possess. Yet, dishonesty seems to be pervasive in our society. Why? I believe the answer lies in these five words of justification: "Everybody else is doing it!"

I remember a front page issue of *U.S. News & World Report* bore this headline: "Lying In America." I also remember reading an article in the *Saturday Evening Post* entitled, "The Honest Truth About Lying."

Post guest author Bob Slosser, a former *New York Times* editor and president of CBN University in Virginia Beach, Virginia, declared: "I fear we have reached the point where lying comes almost as easily as telling the truth. Lying doesn't hurt anymore. Many tend to think that since everyone is cheating, they have to do the same, in order to protect themselves."

Truly, it's a sad state of affairs when lying seems more beneficial than telling the truth. Moreover, dishonesty can never be justified because "everybody else is doing it." Whatever happened to conscience?

A dishonest person always lives a life of unhappiness. Oh, this person may look and act happy on the outside and possess all sorts of tangible symbols of so-called success. Yet, on the inside the cost is a worried mind, a troubled heart and a restless body. Some are bothered more than others. Some may not appear to have any conscience whatsoever. But because their deeds are dishonest, the fear of getting caught always looms on the horizon.

Some people never get caught and the adage that "crime pays" might seem appropriate. Even if these people are never caught by our law enforcement agencies, they're usually caught in the web of their own self-destruction. Some people get caught and their punishment is light because of our lenient justice system. Still others get caught and pay dearly. But always, there is a price to pay and it's only a matter of when and how much.

Honesty, on the other hand, is a long-term investment. By demonstrating this noble quality in their daily living, people reap huge returns. They're known as reliable people. They earn the respect of others. Most importantly, they're shining examples of true success and happiness—a walking testimonial that honesty does pay.

How will you be remembered?

6

Honor

"Success without honor is an unseasoned dish; it will satisfy your hunger, but it won't taste good."
> — *Joe Paterno*
> *Penn State Head Football Coach*

■ ■ ■

Honorable people are successful people whether they ever achieve fame and fortune. Honor is measured by *being* a person of uncompromising character, not by *having* renown and riches.

Honor means being worthy of respect. One of the people I respect the most is my dear friend and running buddy Ron Creasy.

Ron has been an insurance agent for 21 years. His highly successful agency is operated strictly by the book. However, as in any industry, there are always those people who violate company policy to generate more production and income. During his career, Ron has witnessed several agents lose their jobs because of dishonorable behavior. Still, Ron refuses to take short cuts because he places a long-term value upon honor.

We've had numerous training runs in which we've discussed unethical sales practices. Not once has Ron taken the attitude he'd be more successful if he decided to bend or break the rules. He knows that the unscrupulous people are likely to get caught. As a result, they're fired regardless of how many years they've served or how many dollars they've generated.

Ron understands why honor is a series of choices that must be made every day. A bad decision is one that places more importance on short-term financial gain and prestige than long-term honor. A good decision is one that values lifetime respect above the instant gratification of publicity and possessions.

Ron also realizes it's not just what others think of him that counts. Ron is an honorable man because he knows it's the secret to internal contentment. It's possible to deceive others for a while, but it's impossible to fool that familiar face in the mirror each morning. Ron understands what it means to have peace of mind.

Indeed, fame and fortune are fleeting, but honor is passed on from generation to generation. In his own special way, Ron Creasy is a superb business, community and family leader who puts more faith in honor than the size of his ego and wallet. We need more Ron Creasys in this world.

7

Conscience and Personal Responsibility

"There is no witness so dreadful, no accuser so terrible as the conscience that dwells in the heart of man."
— *Polybius*
(2nd Century B.C.)

■ ■ ■

No one should be able to plead ignorance to the rules of ethical conduct. There are Biblical standards such as The Ten Commandments and The Golden Rule. There are business Codes of Ethics. There are federal, state and local laws. There are family rules and regulations.

All of these sources define what ethical (and legal) conduct should be. It's up to each individual to abide by or break these rules. It's a choice each person must make. Out of this choice comes one's lifestyle.

In deciding between a lifestyle of right and wrong or good and bad, the conscience is the guiding force. The conscience, like a computer, is programmed by the value system instilled in us as children. Conscientious people have a high sense of morality and are governed by principle-centered behavior. They act in an ethical manner because of the strong values programmed into their mind.

Unconscientious people have a low sense of morality and are driven by self-centered behavior. They act in an

unethical manner because of the valueless garbage programmed into their minds. Our jails, juvenile homes,
psychiatric wards, hospitals, halfway houses and streets are
full of these people. They're paying a dear price for a weak
conscience and a corrupt value system.

Clearly, we're facing a moral crisis in America. Otherwise, why else would we hear so much talk about family
values and business ethics? What can be done to reverse
this moral decline? How can we do a better job of developing the conscience and value system of our young people?
I believe the answer is found in greater personal responsibility from our adult leadership.

Adult leaders—parents, grandparents, uncles, aunts,
teachers, coaches, ministers, military people, employers and
business executives—must do a better job modeling the
core values advocated in Chapter 1. Children simply won't
program their minds to be ethical if they witness unethical
conduct in adult leaders. Worse yet, if children have no
adult leaders to serve as worthy role models, they'll learn
from their peers. A good example is the explosion of youth
gangs in our urban areas.

No amount of law enforcement agencies or stringent
justice systems can replace conscientious, responsible adult
leaders in our communities. There is no higher calling for
adults than instilling in our young people a sense of
morality, personal responsibility and respect for other
people and their property. As five-star General Omar N.
Bradley observed many years ago, "Ours is a world of
nuclear giants and ethical infants."

8

Trust

"The only way to make a man trustworthy is to trust him; and the surest way to make him untrustworthy is to distrust him and show your distrust."
— *Henry Lewis Stimson*

■ ■ ■

Webster's defines trust as "assured reliance on the character, ability, strength or trust of someone or something." Put another way, trust means to have faith in, to believe in. By nature, Americans are a trusting people.

Trust is fine provided it's a two-way street. But when one party breaks the bond of trust, there can be no meaningful relationship. Trust breeds trust. Mistrust breeds mistrust. Therefore, it's imperative we be careful about the people and organizations we choose to trust.

I remember working with a salesman in the early 1970s whom everyone trusted. He had an effervescent personality, a keen mind and an exceptional sense of humor. He also was the sole provider for a wife and several children. It seemed like he was always short of money. The entire sales force was always loaning him a few dollars. He always paid us back.

This salesman came to me one day in early December. He desperately needed $300, as I recall. I told him that was too much, but agreed to loan him $100. He promised to settle the loan on December 19, which would be timely for

Christmas gifts. When I wrote out that check, I never doubted his word.

On December 19, this salesman said he was in a financial bind and would have my money by January 1. He spent the entire month of January making excuses and giving me the runaround. By early February, he wouldn't return my telephone calls. In short, he had reneged on his promise and broken the trust between us.

Frankly, I would have waited indefinitely for the loan repayment if he had just said, "Dick, I can't pay you for six months, but I *will* pay you." But when he began to lie and avoid me, it was a matter of betrayed trust. I felt compelled to do something. I turned the matter over to a collection agency in February. Three months later, I received a check for $67 after an agency fee of 33%.

I've seen this man twice since that unpleasant experience. He's never mentioned the debt collection. While I hold no animosity toward him, I sincerely hope he learned from this experience. It taught me to value trust as highly as any virtue.

9

Freedom Versus Responsibility

"Freedom isn't free."
— Retired U.S. Army Capt. Tommy Clack
Vietnam veteran and triple amputee

■ ■ ■

In the summer of 1990, there was a controversy over the right to burn the American flag versus a Constitutional amendment to ban flag-burning. It serves as a vivid reminder that all freedoms have a price tag. The price tag on freedom is responsibility.

In America, we enjoy many cherished freedoms, but if we abuse these freedoms, that isn't responsible behavior. For example, consider the following freedom versus responsibility issues:

- ► Americans are free to smoke cigarettes despite the obvious health risks. But if they puff where non-smokers have to inhale this harmful passive smoke, that's not responsible behavior.

- ► Americans are free to drive their automobiles anywhere in this vast nation provided they have the proper documentation. But when they tailgate, zig-zag, speed, cut off other drivers and drive under the influence of alcohol, that's not responsible behavior.

▸ Americans are free to assemble and to speak their minds on vital issues that impact our way of life. But if they take the law into their own hands, that's not responsible behavior.

▸ Americans are free to bear arms for self-defense or recreational uses. But when they walk into a crowded mall or office building and fire at will, that's not responsible behavior.

▸ Americans are free to write their Congressmen about any issues without fear of government reprisal. But when they use the mail to bomb judges and attorneys they disagree with, that's not responsible behavior.

▸ And Americans are free to wave "Old Glory" for whatever reason they choose. But when they burn this symbol of freedom while people from other nations rush to our shores seeking the very freedoms we often take for granted, well, I'm sorry, but that's not responsible behavior.

As Reverend Donald E. Wildman, executive director of the American Family Association, said in a *USA Today* editorial: "Freedom without limits brings chaos. The basic purpose of government is to ensure that civilization, not chaos, rules."

Loyalty

"Loyalty is the basic element which validates and cements relationships."

— Mark Rutland
Hanging By A Thread

■ ■ ■

The word hallmark was an official mark stamped on gold and silver articles in England to indicate their origin, purity and genuineness. It was truly a stamp of approval for value and authenticity used by the jewelers of Goldsmiths' Hall in London. Today, the word hallmark is synonymous with good quality in virtually any product or service.

A hallmark of human qualities is loyalty. It's the bedrock upon which all other character builders are positioned. To be faithful and steadfast in one's allegiance is a noble trait. But in a time of rapid and remarkable change, loyalty seems to be on the wane in three specific areas of our society.

Spiritual Loyalty

America was founded on deep religious principles. One of The Ten Commandments says, "Do not bow down to any idol or worship it, because I am the Lord your God and I tolerate no rivals." (Exodus 20:5, GNV) Yet, in lieu of spiritual loyalty, this nation seems to be preoccupied with excessive indulgence in cleverly disguised idols such as greed, lust and pride (see Chapters 16-18).

Isn't it ironic that in a nation blessed with the freedom of religion, so many have taken it for granted? Millions of Americans don't attend church regularly. Millions don't read the Bible regularly. Millions have refused to become involved in social issues while active minorities have influenced the Supreme Court to strike down prayer in our schools and legalize abortion. Are we far away from removing the words "under God" from our flag's pledge of allegiance?

Marital Loyalty

Society seems quite tolerant of extramarital affairs as long as "you don't get caught." This permissiveness is undermining the very fabric of our society—the family unit as the basis for teaching sound moral principles. A faithful commitment is what enables a marriage to grow. "Fidelity," said Emil Brunner, "is the ethical element which enhances natural love."

I'm not suggesting change (divorce) should never be considered. Every marriage experiences some tough choices over a lifetime. Sometimes divorce is the best and perhaps the only sensible solution, especially in cases of infidelity or physical abuse. However, the grass isn't always greener on the proverbial "other side." Perhaps the greatest joy in marital loyalty is the team satisfaction of overcoming life's many trials, tribulations and temptations to improve the relationship we already have.

Employer Loyalty

Due to hostile takeovers, mergers, acquisitions and tough economic times, employer loyalty certainly isn't what it used to be. Employees are a lot less likely to spend their entire career with one employer. They simply don't believe their loyalty will be rewarded.

The gold watch, long a symbol of company fidelity, has been badly tarnished with the erosion of employer loyalty. Somehow, we need to restore the dignity of employer loyalty to the American worker. Somehow, we need to give our high school, technical school and college graduates more hope that their years of education will not be in vain. They need to know their meaningful contributions will be rewarded with steady, long-term employment.

Loyalty transcends short-term problems and challenges in pursuit of long-term growth and happiness. Is loyalty the hallmark of your character?

11

Sincerity

*"It cannot be over-emphasized that nothing, absolutely
nothing, can take the place of sincerity in a speaker."*
— *Dr. Kenneth McFarland*
Eloquence In Public Speaking

■ ■ ■

Dr. McFarland was one of the great orators of the 20th
century. While his book refers to sincerity in public
speakers, everyone is a public speaker through their
behavior. A person simply can't say one thing, do another
and be taken sincerely.

The indispensable quality of sincerity is what enables a
person to "walk their talk." The opposite of sincerity is
hypocrisy. A hypocrite is a pretender or, as the American
Indian would say, a person who "speaks with forked
tongue."

Sincerity comes from the heart but is expressed outwardly
with the same genuineness. There's a certain warmth
radiated by a sincere heart, a warmth that makes a person
believable. "You were sincere and believable" are the
highest words of praise an audience can share with me after
a speaking or training engagement.

Dr. Norman Vincent Peale is a man of great sincerity.
My wife, good friend Ken Futch and I had the opportunity
to meet Dr. Peale and his lovely wife, Ruth, on July 24,
1990. He was the closing speaker at the annual convention

of the National Speakers Association. As president of the host Georgia Speakers Association, it was my job to meet this charming couple at the Atlanta Airport.

A spry 92 at the time, I asked Dr. Peale if he'd ever considered retirement. "No," he answered, "I just keep on keeping on." So, I asked him why he still works at such an advanced age. "Well," Dr. Peale remarked with a twinkle in his eye, "there are still a few negative thinkers around."

I was amazed to learn he was still rising at 5:30 a.m., going to the office regularly and delivering about 60-70 talks per year at an age most of us will never see. And, of course, he's the author of 34 books, including *The Power Of Positive Thinking*, and hundreds of magazine articles.

Perhaps the real mark of his sincerity is his devotion to the thousands of people who have benefited from his words of wisdom. His office staff of 130 handles about 8,000 letters per day and "we try to answer them all," said Dr. Peale. "I like short letters."

This living legend, a man standing about 5'5", was gracious enough to autograph one of his books for me. A week later, a remarkable thing happened. I received a short letter from Norman Vincent Peale that ended sincerely: "And God bless you and Judy." It now hangs proudly on my office wall.

12

Love

"Meanwhile, these three remain: faith, hope, and love; and the greatest of these is love."
— *I Corinthians 13:13 (GNV)*

■　■　■

Perhaps the greatest words ever written about love are found in the 13th chapter of Paul's letter to the Corinthians. Unfortunately, some 2,000 years later, the world still struggles with the true meaning of love.

When Jesus was asked to name the most important commandments, he replied: "Love the Lord your God with all your heart, with all your soul, with all your mind, and with all your strength. The second most important commandment is this: Love your neighbor as you love yourself." (Mark 12:30-31, GNV)

It's no coincidence Jesus refers to the love of God, love of others and love of self in that order. His entire life was an unselfish message of love, including his death on the cross as an atonement for the sins of humankind. Let's look at the following three expressions of love as the foundation for being a person of impeccable character and meaningful purpose.

Love of God

We show our love for God in many ways. Worship services are important. Daily prayers are important. Regular Bible reading and study are important. Perhaps the best way we show our love for God is by obeying His laws in our daily living.

Love of Others

In I John 4:20 (GNV) it says: "If someone says he loves God, but hates his brother, he is a liar. For he cannot love God, whom he has not seen, if he does not love his brother, whom he has seen." We are made in God's image. Since God is a loving God, he commands us to love one another. Yet, the world is full of malice, jealousy, revenge and hate and we wonder why world peace is so elusive.

Love of Self

We should show our love of self not in a conceited manner, but rather in the grateful ways we maintain our mind, body and spirit as we strive to honor God and serve others. When we fail to stimulate our minds with worthwhile thoughts and deeds, that's inappropriate self love. When we fail to maintain our bodies by not observing preventive health measures, that's inappropriate self love. When we fail to feed our souls with the spirit of God, that's inappropriate self love.

It takes no special race, religion, nationality, education, social status, financial means or job title to express love. Love is the universal language everyone speaks, so why isn't it spoken more freely and frequently? Maybe it's because love is difficult to define. Yet, love becomes abundantly clear when demonstrated.

The word love may be used as a noun or a verb. Nouns are persons, places or things. Indeed, love is a good thing. Verbs express action. When love is expressed beyond words and into deeds, it is more than a good thing. It is the difference between war and peace; the difference between failure and success; the difference between simply existing and really living; and the difference between disillusionment and hope.

Yes, the power of love is truly miraculous if we'll only demonstrate it more often and openly.

13

Humility

"It has been said that one who has humility doesn't know it. I once heard a man brag about having humility."
— *Dolph Braddy*
Thoughts In Maturity

■ ■ ■

You've probably heard the expression, "That person is a legend in their own time." But have you ever known someone who was a "legend in their own *mind*"? Regardless of their accomplishments, no one is so good that a healthy dose of humility will not make them great.

The late Robert W. Woodruff was a wonderful example of a man who possessed great riches, fame, power and humility. The longtime chairman of The Coca-Cola Company gave away millions of dollars, including a donation of $105 million to Emory University in 1980. It's the largest single gift ever made to an educational institution.

Despite his enormous generosity, Woodruff was known as "Mr. Anonymous" for years before gradually permitting his name to be identified with his benevolences. While Woodruff enjoyed helping others, he didn't seek a lot of fanfare for his philanthropy. Today, Robert Woodruff is memorialized all over Georgia and elsewhere. This highly successful businessman is remembered as a humble philanthropist, not as a rich, selfish and arrogant tycoon.

Perhaps humility is one of life's most difficult lessons to learn. It's only natural to desire recognition for our accomplishments and to take pride in a job well done. The problem seems to arise when we become overly enamored with our successes.

Humility is the quality that enables us to seek excellence while realizing success is never achieved alone. Truly great leaders always give credit to their people. Truly great ball players always give credit to their teammates. Truly great citizens always give credit to their families, schools, employers, country and God.

Robert Woodruff was that kind of team player. He kept a bronze plaque in his office that said, "There is no limit to what a man can do or where he can go if he doesn't mind who gets the credit." New employees of Coca-Cola still receive a pamphlet Woodruff was particularly fond of—"It's Human Relations That Count." The following words from that pamphlet provide insight into the humility of Woodruff: "The basic rule of good human relations is to think, talk and act in terms of the interest of the other person. It is to get one's thinking off one's self and one's own little world and of directing it to the other person."

No one enjoys being around an egomaniac. It makes us feel like our contributions are insignificant, that someone else is taking undue credit. Be the best you can be, but let others sing your praises. Always keep your achievements in the proper perspective by heeding the words of Jesus in Matthew 23:12 (GNV): "Whoever makes himself great will be humbled, and whoever humbles himself will be made great."

14

Patience

"When you have patience, you realize that if you do what is right—even if it costs you in the short run—it will pay off in the long run."
— *Kenneth Blanchard & Norman Vincent Peale*
The Power Of Ethical Management

■ ■ ■

I wrote my original business plan on October 8, 1979. I didn't launch my company until October 4, 1982. Those three years taught me a lot about patience.

Like many people, I often struggle with patience. I like to get things done. Obviously, a certain sense or urgency (or impatience, if you will) is necessary to get things done. However, as I've matured, I've discovered patience is often the gradual learning process that allows us to see, in time, the big picture of life.

In 1979, I couldn't see the big picture. All I could see was the excitement of owning an automobile leasing company. Since I only had two years of leasing experience and was woefully short of investment capital, I wrote my business plan to include two partners. Ken Tapp, a friend since my teenage years and a man I recruited into the automobile business in 1971, would be my working partner. Sonny Bonner, Ken's brother-in-law, would be our financial partner.

Ken and I arranged a meeting with Sonny. We took our seven-page business plan to that meeting expecting Sonny to say yes to our ambitious proposal. Sonny rejected our idea with good reason. In retrospect, I now know he did us a big favor by saying no.

The early 1980s was a time of astronomical inflation and interest rates. It was not a particularly good time to be opening a business. If we had failed, Sonny would have taken a big financial loss. Moreover, I was a bachelor with minimal expenses. Ken was married, had two small children and a big mortgage. Undoubtedly, those differences could have strained our relationship.

What I discovered in the three-year period between writing my business plan and implementing it was that patience is the ultimate teacher. I never gave up on my dream during those three years. In fact, I became more determined than ever. By 1982, I had three more years of leasing experience, a broader base of customers, some capital of my own and a better business climate.

If patience is anything, it's learning to endure. If endurance is anything, it's understanding the importance of timing. In 1979, the timing simply wasn't right for my business. Through patience and endurance, I kept my dream alive until the timing improved. Most of all, I learned that patience should never become a routine substitute for habitual procrastination.

15

Role Models

"Everyday leaders influence us as much as world leaders because they act as role models and set examples for us on a much more personal level."
— *Sheila Murray Bethel*
Making A Difference

■ ■ ■

Eva Bullington Hall, my maternal grandmother, was a splendid example of an everyday leader who served as a quiet but effective role model. She lived most of her life in rural Newport, Tennessee. She had little formal education, was a housewife all of her adult life and had few material possessions.

Grandmother Hall lived through four wars, the Great Depression, the accidental death of her youngest child (my Aunt Edith) and the agonizingly slow death of her husband Samuel Joseph Hall. At Grandfather Hall's funeral, she made us promise to visit as soon as possible. Six months later, my wife and I returned—the weekend of June 22-23, 1985. We had originally scheduled our visit for the following weekend, but changed the time at the last minute.

Though still grieving the loss of her husband of 62 years, my grandmother seemed healthy and alert. The Sunday morning before we left—June 23, 1985 and exactly two months before her 80th birthday—we sat on her front porch with the majestic Great Smoky Mountains in view.

We talked about the family tree. Grandmother proudly recited some six generations while I took careful notes.

Finally, she gazed confidently at me, the oldest of her eight grandchildren, and said: "Dick, I haven't been real successful in life. I haven't done a lot of things, gone a lot of places or had a lot of money. But if I've done nothing else, I've tried to raise my three children the best way I knew how by setting a good example for them and all you grandchildren." We left about an hour later to return home to Atlanta. Grandmother waved a tearful farewell.

When we walked into our home that Sunday evening, the telephone was ringing. It was my mother. "Dick," she said slowly, "I have some bad news. Your grandmother died of a massive stroke about an hour after you left. You were the last ones to see her alive." As we drove back to Newport for the funeral a couple of days later, I was thinking about two things.

First, I was relieved we'd changed the date of our visit. More importantly, I had this calming thought. Grandmother Hall, you were a success more than you'll ever know. You had honesty and integrity and you modeled these worthwhile qualities for the people that mattered most to you in life—your children and grandchildren.

On that memorable day—June 23, 1985—I learned a most valuable lesson. Exemplary role models don't have to have fame, formal education and fortune to be effective. They simply need to practice honesty and integrity as a way of life. It's impossible not to model. I'm just grateful Grandmother Hall chose to be a positive role model.

16

Money: A Perspective

"Riches are apt to betray a man into arrogance."
— Thomas Addison

■ ■ ■

Most immoral or illegal behavior can be traced to three character demolishers—the abuse of money, sex and power. This chapter will discuss money and chapters 17 and 18 will deal with sex and power.

The major problem with money is greed! The Bible does not say money is evil, but rather "the love of money is a source of all kinds of evil." (I Timothy 6:10, GNV) It is humankind's excessive love of money that leads to greed, which seems to bring out the worst in people.

The opposite of greed is generosity or a willingness to share what we accumulate in life and what we certainly can't take with us in death. Greed or generosity is all a matter of perspective. Will riches be used in a selfish and corrupt manner or in a caring and well-intentioned fashion?

Greed is a no-win proposition since no amount of money is ever sufficient. While it's quite natural to desire wealth, the challenge, as suggested by Richard J. Foster in *Money, Sex & Power*, is "to use money within the confines of a properly disciplined life and to manage money for the good of all humanity and for the glory of God."

On the other hand, a spirit of generosity understands everything we have belongs to God. Our challenge is to manage whatever we've been entrusted with in a grateful and loving way. A generous person loves people and uses money wisely. A greedy person loves money and uses people in the insatiable pursuit of materialism.

If money could ensure happiness, every rich person would be happy. King Solomon, considered the wisest man who ever lived, sought success and happiness in materialism and vanity. He concluded near the end of his life, "When I turned to look at all I had achieved and at all my efforts and trouble, then it was all vain and futile . . . all was vanity and a striving after wind." (Ecclesiastes 2:11, GNV)

Remember, money is a matter of perspective. When great wealth is coupled with a generous spirit, it enriches our world. When riches and greed become partners, it becomes a losing relationship for everyone.

17

Sex: A Perspective

"Sex, sex, sex! How can anything so beautiful become the focus of so much ugly conflict in America?"
— *Carl Rowan*

■ ■ ■

The major problem with sex is lust! The newspapers and magazines are full of stories about adultery, pornography, sexual diseases, rape, abortion, incest, homosexuality and prostitution. And television uses sexy commercials because "sex sells."

Since the American sexual revolution exploded in the 1960s, we've witnessed a moral collapse unparalleled in our nation's history. With sexual abuses so rampant, is it any wonder why we have such a serious moral decline in our society? Is lust out of control?

Like so many problems, the solution usually lies in a return to the basics. In I Corinthians 6:19 (GNV), we're given some wise advice about our bodies: "Don't you know that your body is the temple of the Holy Spirit, who lives in you and who was given to you by God? You do not belong to yourselves but to God."

Unquestionably, our sexuality is a part of our humanness. How we use this sexuality is a choice everyone must make. We can take the hedonistic view that pleasure, and especially lust, is the sole good in life. Or we can take the hallowed approach and treat sexuality as a sacred and special relationship.

It seems our permissive society has embraced the hedonistic view towards sexuality. Those who take the hallowed approach are labeled as "puritanical" and "old-fashioned." I believe it's time to turn the tide on the sexual revolution and return to more responsible behavior.

When teenage sexual activity, pregnancies and abortions are widespread, it's time to make some changes. When convicted rapists often spend only a short time in jail, it's time to make some changes. When AIDS is a national epidemic, it's time to make some changes. And when adultery and homosexuality are accepted as "normal" behavior, it's time to make some changes.

I'm not talking about legislating moral behavior. If sexual conduct is to change for the better, adult leadership at all levels of society must change by serving as worthy role models for our youth. Children must be taught, primarily by example, that sexuality and personal responsibility are partners. Kids need to understand that a lustful, irresponsible lifestyle has dire consequences; and that a hallowed approach towards sexuality has favorable, long-term rewards for each person in particular and society in general.

Lust prevents healthy relationships from growing because it treats people like objects. Without strong relationships, a society is without a solid foundation. The strongest relationship is a faithful marriage between man and woman. Marriage is God's institution for an intimate relationship, including sexuality, and provides the framework for building strong families.

The distorted view of sexuality (lust) that is now so pervasive must be changed to a more caring and responsible attitude between the sexes. Otherwise, the "ugly conflict" referenced by Carl Rowan could become our modern day Sodom and Gomorrah.

18

Power: A Perspective

*"It is regretted that the rich and powerful too often
bend the acts of government for their selfish purposes."*
— *Andrew Jackson*

■ ■ ■

The major problem with power is pride! Leaders often
use their influential positions to exult themselves rather
than serve their people. Excessive pride generally results
in abusive leadership.

Thus, the wise use of power becomes a matter of self
versus service. In serving others, leaders are also served and
everyone wins. If power is used for selfish purposes,
leaders do immeasurable damage to themselves, the people
around them and everyone loses.

Power can be wonderfully constructive or incredibly
destructive. Destructive power manifests itself though an
intense desire to dominate others. The will of the leader is
imposed upon others for the sake of inflating the leader's
ego and reputation. Adolf Hitler was such a leader and it
led to his downfall and death.

By contrast, constructive power manifests itself through
a genuine respect for other people and their concerns. This
type of leader finds out what the people want, then serves
as a guide in the accomplishment of these goals. Franklin
Delano Roosevelt was such a leader and it kept him in

office as President of the United States for a record 12 years.

Pride is a quality every good leader must possess, but it must be tempered with humility or the power scale becomes unbalanced. Leaders with inordinate amounts of self-esteem manage to take all the credit for "their" accomplishments. Humble leaders put the spotlight on others rather than basking in the glow of their leadership skills.

I once heard Jeane Kirkpatrick, a former U.S. Ambassador to the United States and distinguished scholar, deliver a speech on the history of leadership. She recited fascinating stories about many famous leaders, but I'll always remember her closing comment: "People generally get the leadership they deserve."

One notable reason for the success of the United States is its understanding of power. Leaders who become too proud don't get re-elected. The real power is not in the hands of the leaders, but in the minds of the people. That's why the Preamble of the U.S. Constitution starts off with, "We the people." That's why Abraham Lincoln ended his Gettysburg Address with these stirring words: ". . . and that government of the people, by the people, for the people, shall not perish from this earth."

It's no coincidence that greed, lust and pride are the character demolishers at the root of most unethical and illegal behavior. That's why the character builders described in Chapters 1-14 are so vital to being a commendable role model.

19

Faith

"To have faith is to be sure of the things we hope for, to be certain of the things we cannot see."
— *Hebrews 11:1 (GNV)*

■ ■ ■

Faith provides the strength that holds a person to the right purpose in life. Yet, the very word faith is defined in Webster's as a "firm belief in something for which there is no proof." So how is it possible to have a powerful life's purpose based upon something that can't be proven?

It's important to understand faith is a spiritual thing, not a physical thing that can be seen and proven. I choose to have faith in God even though I've never seen God. Nevertheless, God's proof is everywhere—in the creation of humankind; in a beautiful sunrise or sunset; in the harmony of the ocean tides; in the majestic mountains and lush green valleys; in the rains and bountiful farm lands that supply our food and drink; and, yes, in His inspired word, The Holy Bible.

To those who believe the universe merely evolved, I cite the words of Dr. Ken Boa, who calls evolution the "greatest myth of our time." To those who say, "It doesn't matter what you believe as long as you sincerely believe in something," I strongly disagree. It does matter what you believe. Unless one's purpose conforms to the Divine Laws of God and observes a high standard of moral values, there can be no worthwhile purpose.

Faith involves some degree of risk since it's an intangible. In fact, Dr. Robert Schuller says that "faith is impossible without risk." Small children are great examples. Their very existence depends upon the care of parents and loved ones. Children place their unconditional trust in adults until they can provide for themselves.

Likewise, we are God's children. He calls for us to be true to His ways, but we're given the free will to choose between good and evil. Have you chosen to place your spiritual allegiance in God or is your mental, physical and emotional faith in the ways of the world? The world beckons to us through our five senses. God calls us through the spiritual link of faith.

Anyone who treats faith in God like a science is missing the very essence of faith. It can't be put under a microscope or demonstrated like the theory of gravity. It's a conviction that's felt on the inside and moves mountains on the outside.

Without faith in God, there is no spiritual inner strength to endure or to cope with the struggles of life. When we don't trust God, there is no hope for a better life. However, with faith in God, all things are possible. Remember, what you believe creates the life you choose to live. What do you believe?

Purpose

> *"The only purposes that will survive are ones linked to God."*
>
> — *Patrick M. Morley*
> The Man In The Mirror

■　■　■

Absolute Faith In the Right Purpose
by Dick Biggs

You must possess a worthwhile purpose
If true success is to be achieved.
A sublime mission, a better way of life
Becomes a guiding force to be believed.

Purpose determines your direction in life
Are you going where you want to go?
Don't be betrayed by meaningless goals
The right purpose will help you grow.

Beware of excessive fondness for vanity
Because fame is likely to pass you by.
Alas, fortune offers no lasting guarantee
Regardless of how hard you try.

Love your fellow man, serve him well
To unlock the door to real happiness.
Place your absolute faith in God
And you'll be blessed with true success.

Purpose Versus Goals

"A goal is not a purpose. A goal is something tangible. It is something definite you can accomplish. It has a beginning and an end. A purpose is ongoing. It gives meaning and definition to our lives."
— *Kenneth Blanchard & Norman Vincent Peale*
The Power of Ethical Management

■ ■ ■

There's a lot of emphasis on goal-setting and rightly so. But goals are simply lists of activities to do or things to have. Purpose has more noble significance. It's a reflection of who a person is.

Purpose provides direction in life. Direction comes from having absolute faith in the right purpose. The key question is, "What is the right purpose for my life?" Many people maintain "to do" and "to have" lists, but what about their life's purpose in writing?

Goals, while always changing, are easier to put in writing because they're tangible. It's a lot more difficult to put your life's purpose on paper. It requires long-range thinking and a sorting out of what's important.

To develop a personal statement of purpose (or mission) requires a rigid self-examination of one's beliefs. Are these beliefs based on greed, power, lust, anger and hate? Or are these beliefs based on faith in God, loving and serving others and genuine self-improvement?

Surrendering to a worthwhile purpose does not mean personal goals shouldn't be pursued. To the contrary, focusing on the intimate and examined purpose can lead to a richer, fuller life. Superiority of purpose places faith in God and concern for others above self. Superiority of purpose understands the Law of Reciprocity gives back 10 times more than is given.

Benjamin Disraeli said "the secret of success is constancy to purpose." I'd like to paraphrase that great quote by saying the secret to *true* success is constancy to the *right* purpose. For me, the right purpose is God-centered, people-oriented and self-improvement conscious—in that order!

A meaningful purpose provides the strength and direction to live a life of true success and happiness. The power of purpose should never be underestimated since it determines the road you choose to travel in life. Romans 8:28 (GNV) says it well: "We know that in all things God works for good with those who love Him, those whom He has called according to His purpose."

What is your purpose in life? Do you have it in writing?

22

Personal Mission Statement

"You could call a personal mission statement a personal constitution. Like the United States Constitution, it's fundamentally changeless."

— *Steven Covey*
The Seven Habits Of Highly Effective People

■ ■ ■

Here's my personal mission statement:

1. I will strive to maintain my *integrity* in all facets of my daily living.

2. I will strive to have a positive *impact* upon the people whose lives I touch; and to set a worthy example to all as an honest and principle-centered role model.

3. I will strive to honor God in all I think, say and do. I realize how I live on earth, coupled with my belief in Jesus Christ as my personal Savior, will lead to *immortality* with God in heaven.

Out of that statement of purpose (or mission) came a list of three dominant interests which create a reasonable measure of balance in my life. Notice that God and my spiritual life form the hub of my being. Observe how the dominant interests pertaining to others and self are centered around my religious faith:

I—God/Spiritual:

► This covers my faith in God, daily devotions, tithing to my church and other charities, teaching Sunday school and trying to set a worthy Christian example each day in all areas of my life.

II—Others:

► *Family*—This means spending time with my wife, stepdaughters and other family members.

► *Friends*—This is a selective list because truly good friends are rare.

► *Community*—This includes involvement in various civic activities.

III—Personal:

► *Business*—This focuses on running my business and participating in two professional associations.

- *Finances*—This takes in the family budget, savings, investments, insurance, banking, tax and estate planning, etc.

- *Health/Leisure*—This encompasses my physical fitness program, proper diet and rest, regular medical and dental exams, and time for activities such as vacations, sporting events, reading and hobbies.

My personal mission statement enables me to focus on these dominant interests. I then set goals (Chapter 34) and daily priorities (Chapter 35) within each of these dominant interests to help me stay on track. There is never perfect harmony, to be sure, but there is a reasonable measure of balance.

One final suggestion: If you don't have a personal mission statement, I encourage you to develop one with a minimal number of dominant interests. As Everett T. Suters, an Atlanta-based speaker, consultant and writer, says: "When we attempt to focus on everything, we haven't focused on anything."

23

Business Mission Statement

"1. To glorify God by being a faithful steward of all that is entrusted to us. 2. To have a positive influence on all who come in contact with Chick-fil-A."
— *Corporate Purpose of Chick-fil-A*
Atlanta, Georgia

■ ■ ■

In *It's Easier To Succeed Than To Fail*, Chick-fil-A founder and CEO S. Truett Cathy tells how their corporate purpose (or mission) statement came about with sales declining in the 1982 recession. Cathy called a meeting of his executive staff at Pine Isle Hotel on Lake Lanier, an hour north of his Atlanta-based headquarters. Several gut-wrenching hours later, the above two sentences were completed to signify why Chick-fil-A is in business.

I generally ask the attendees of my leasing seminars, "What's your purpose for being in business?" The answer is almost always "to make money!" There's no denying a company has to make a profit to stay in business. But making money is not the purpose of my business. My company's purpose (or mission) is to serve my customers the best way I can.

Now, I'll admit a shortage of money has been a serious concern on many occasions since going into business in

1982. However, I've never wavered from my purpose even when the cash flow wasn't flowing. Somehow, the money always seems to come when it's needed the most. Truly, God has seen fit to provide for my company in some mighty dark hours.

My attitude has always been that if a business is really customer-focused, the money will follow. That doesn't mean I won't have to work hard or I won't have some down times. It doesn't guarantee I'll always be in business. But as long as I'm in business, I intend to operate by the following creed:

Business Mission Statement of Biggs Automobile Leasing Corporation:

1. I will strive to maintain my integrity in all my business relationships.

2. I will strive to deliver honest, professional advice and quality personal service to all my customers.

3. I will strive to honor God in all my business transactions as a shining example to others of my Christian faith and commitment.

The Biblical foundation for that statement came from Micah 6:8 (GNV): ". . . the Lord has told us what is good. What he requires of us is this: to do what is just, to show constant love, and to live in humble fellowship with our God."

Why is your company in business? More importantly, is there a conflict between what you believe and the way your company does business?

24

Business Ethics

"The only sacred cow in an organization is its princi-
ples. A company must never change them. No matter
what its nature or size, there must be certain bedrock
beliefs to serve as its guiding force."

— *Buck Rodgers*
The IBM Way

■ ■ ■

I was once asked this haunting question after conducting
an automobile leasing seminar: "Is it possible to maintain
personal integrity and still survive in the highly competitive
automobile business?"

Before delving into that question, here's what an automobile dealership general manager once told me: "Dick, I'll be
ethical if I can. But if competition forces me to do otherwise, I'll do whatever it takes."

It's impossible to separate personal integrity and business
ethics. A corporate Code of Ethics is no better than the
individual moral behavior of each employee. An ethical
business requires ethical employees.

This "I'll be ethical if I can" approach to doing business
represents ethical compromise, which undermines the very
meaning of integrity. To truly succeed in business, high
ethical standards must be observed consistently. Otherwise,
the unethical conduct of a single employee becomes the

weak link in the company chain, a situation that can destroy the credibility and longevity of a business.

Indeed, business owners must lead the way by living up to the high standards of the corporate Code of Ethics. There is absolutely no excuse for immoral or amoral leadership. For the moral leader, there is no greater satisfaction than doing business in an ethical manner.

Immoral leaders—the ones who are always doing unethical things—are doomed to failure. Amoral leaders—the ones who compromise their integrity when they deem necessary—are eventually destroyed by their own intricate web of deceit. Moral leaders know doing the right thing consistently is in the best interest of the leader, the employees, the company, the customers and the overall business community.

So is it possible to maintain personal integrity and survive, even thrive, in an intensely competitive business environment? The answer is a definite yes because short-term ethical compromise by any employee jeopardizes the long-term success of the company. As speaker Ken Futch is fond of saying, "You can shear a sheep many times, but you can only skin it once!"

25

Goodness

"If we live good lives, the times are also good. As we are, such are the times."

— *St. Augustine*

■ ■ ■

We hear a lot about living the "good life." However, the so-called good life and living a life filled with goodness are often at extreme ends of the balance beam of life. So what is the good life?

In today's permissive society, the "good life" is often envisioned as one full of money, sex and power as discussed in chapters 16, 17 and 18. In reality, the abuse of money (greed), sex (lust) and power (pride) often provide an abundance of problems rather than an abundantly good life. Alas, the good life doesn't have to be so perplexing.

On the contrary, the good life is a striving for real goodness. Obviously, the risk in seeking this particular lifestyle is being branded as self-righteous. While none of us should feel like our beliefs make us any better than those with contrasting beliefs, it's really a matter of answering two simple but profound questions: Who am I? Why do I exist?

The first 24 chapters of this "To Be" section were written to help anyone do a better job answering these difficult questions in pursuit of a more balanced lifestyle. A person of goodness knows the answer to "Who am I?"

is found in a value system based upon such qualities as integrity, honesty, honor, conscience, accountability, trust, responsibility, loyalty, sincerity, love, humility and patience. While these noble qualities are simple in theory, they're never easy to practice in daily living.

Furthermore, a person of goodness knows the answer to "Why do I exist?" is based upon a purpose dedicated to honoring God, serving humanity and living up to one's full potential. The personal and business mission statements (chapters 22 and 23) bring this worthwhile purpose into clear focus. For anyone struggling with their life's purpose—and most of us do—ask yourself this soul-searching question: When I look back upon my life, will I be proud of what it stood for?

A life of goodness doesn't mean being better than everyone else. It merely means being different. In striving to be a person of noble character and purpose, it's inevitable these differences will be ridiculed. But I'd rather be ridiculed for seeking a life of goodness than be remorseful at life's end because the so-called good life wasn't so good after all.

Time put this whole matter of goodness versus the good life in perspective: "In place of materialism, many Americans are embracing simpler pleasures and homier values. They've been thinking hard about what really matters in their lives, and they've decided to make some changes. What matters is having time for family and friends, rest and recreation, good deeds and spirituality."

PART II

"TO THINK"

The Mental Force

"We become what we think about."
— *Earl Nightingale*
Earl Nightingale's Greatest Discovery

26

Imagination

"Imagination is more important than knowledge."
— Albert Einstein

■ ■ ■

I spent my last two years in the Marine Corps as a security guard at the American embassies in Warsaw and Rome. Those two years were as different as day and night. One was spent behind the Iron Curtain, the other in a free country.

While in Poland, I learned the value of imagination and creativity. We were fairly restricted due to security reasons, so I had a lot of free time. I began to brainstorm about the ways I could sharpen my writing skills to be ready to resume my journalistic career when I returned to Atlanta.

I enrolled in a two-year correspondence course in non-fiction writing. I conducted a poll of America's 50 largest newspapers to determine which sports writers were considered the best by their peers. I received 39 responses and compiled a list of the top 10 sports writers. Since the embassy library subscribed to many of these newspapers, I was able to read most of the great sports writers each week.

It wasn't uncommon for me to rewrite the columns of such legendary sports writers as Red Smith, Dick Young, Arthur Daley, Furman Bisher, Fred Russell, Jim Murray and Jack Murphy. That took imagination! But I wanted to develop my own style, so I tore apart some great writing for the sake of creativity.

Furthermore, I spent hours imagining what it would be like when I returned to the journalistic firing line. I'd write lead paragraphs and pretend I only had five minutes before the deadline. I was preparing mentally for what I fully expected to happen.

That experience taught me how imaginative one mind can be. I've since learned that several minds engaged in a collective brainstorming session can be even more powerful and creative. While the Bible (Ecclesiastes 1:9, NIV) says that "there's nothing new under the sun," I'm convinced there are always new ways to implement old ideas.

In *Law Of Success*, Napoleon Hill summed up his feelings on imagination this way: "The imagination is the workshop of the human mind whereby old ideas and established facts may be reassembled into new combinations and put to new uses."

27

Awareness

"Hold every moment sacred. Give each clarity and meaning, each the weight of thine awareness, each its true and due fulfillment."

— *Thomas Mann*
The Beloved Returns

■ ■ ■

Perhaps the greatest gift a parent or any other adult leader can give a child is an awareness of how powerful learning can be. One of the best ways to create such an awareness is through travel. Fortunately, my family was always going somewhere.

As a result of our travels, I developed a boyhood awareness of maps. This awareness led to a desire to learn to read maps. Eventually, my father trusted my map reading ability enough to put me in charge of coordinating the routes for our trips.

We visited a lot of historic places. In particular, I became fascinated by Civil War history. I began to collect and read books about this era. By the time I entered college, I had more than 200 volumes on the Civil War. I could discuss the major battles and leaders in vivid detail.

Thankfully, my parents were always encouraging me to read, to appreciate good literature and the lessons to be learned. They used to catch me reading late at night under the covers with the aid of a flashlight. I became such an

avid reader that my mother had to force me outside to play
ball with the neighborhood kids.

I'm grateful to my parents for providing an awareness
of quality learning. In turn, this awareness helped shape the
direction of my life. Strong academic awareness usually
becomes the foundation for a meaningful life. Weak
academic awareness often results in an unproductive,
wasted life. Clearly, it's a choice that shouldn't be taken
lightly.

I'm convinced adult leaders must do more to enhance
the value of academic awareness for the young people in
their care. Otherwise, we'll continue to witness kids
replacing school with gangs, drug dealing, violence, larceny
and other illegal activities.

Of course, it isn't difficult to understand why many
children struggle with an awareness of quality education.
Besides negligent adult leadership, consider the outside
influences. Commercials tell our kids it's okay to drink
alcohol. Advertisers tell our young people smoking is a
cool thing to do. Movies are full of sex, violence and lewd
language. Shallow television shows steal valuable hours
from productive learning time.

In order for children to become more aware of the long-
term value of quality education, adult leaders must create
better learning environments. Advertisers, movie and
television producers and the media must be more responsible with the messages they convey to our youth. Private
enterprise must become more involved in this academic
awareness crisis. After all, the pursuit of quality education
begins with awareness.

28

Knowledge

"That there should one man die ignorant who had capacity for knowledge, this I call a tragedy."
— *Thomas Carlyle*
Sartor Resartus

■ ■ ■

If we're fortunate enough to be provided the proper *awareness* of learning as discussed in Chapter 27, there are three significant points to consider in the quest for knowledge.

First, it's necessary to understand the accumulation and understanding of knowledge is a *process*. One body of knowledge builds upon another body in the same way one floor builds upon another floor in the erection of a skyscraper. Literally, we are building a skyscraper of knowledge one day at a time. Thomas Macaulay, a 19th century English historian, understood this process well by noting, "Knowledge advances by steps, not by leaps."

As a result of this process, we must dedicate ourselves to be life-long learners. We must always be looking to learn. We must continually seek out good books, inspirational tapes, educational seminars and positive, experienced people willing to share their knowledge. That's why school is never out for people who want to grow and prosper.

Second, a part of this process is *repetition*. The mind is the greatest computer ever conceived, but it has to be used to be effective. Study is crucial. As Dr. Samuel Johnson once observed, "The number of new things a man needs to learn is less important than the number of old things he needs to be reminded of."

I'm grateful to Eloise Penn, a high school English teacher, newspaper adviser and speech coach, for her repetitious nature. Whether we were diagramming sentences, discussing a book, writing an article or preparing for a speech, Miss Penn was relentless in her teaching approach. She believed practice was the essential key to understanding and retaining knowledge. Woe be it to any student who wasn't properly prepared.

Third, the learning process is necessary for us to discover our *direction* (or purpose) in life. Plato once said, "Untaught we cannot look in the right direction." Truly, an inquiring mind is a precious gift, but a focused mind is a powerful manifestation of that gift.

The gift of learning enables us to choose how we'll apply our education towards a meaningful life's purpose, which will be discussed further in Chapter 29. General knowledge opens our eyes to the numerous journeys we can take in life. Specific knowledge allows us to concentrate on a more pinpointed direction as we pursue more fulfilling and rewarding careers by *applying* what we know to a field of expertise.

29

Applied Knowledge

"Knowledge is only potential power. It becomes power only when, and if, organized into definite plans of action and directed to a definite end."
— *Napoleon Hill*
Think And Grow Rich

■ ■ ■

"Debut Into A World Of Realities" was the title of my graduation speech to the 1963 class of East Atlanta High School in Atlanta, Georgia. I suggested the learning triangle has three sides—the accumulation, understanding and application of knowledge—and our learning up to that point had been primarily concerned with the first two steps.

"We have had limited opportunities to apply our learning to the various experiences of life," I said to my fellow classmates. "It is now our obligation not only to continue the accumulation and understanding of knowledge, but also to apply this learning in the real world. As a basis for applied learning, we must depend upon purpose. Therefore, it's imperative that we understand the relationship between knowledge and purpose."

Unfortunately, I failed to follow my own lofty advice at the tender age of 17. Oh, I continued to accumulate and understand a lot of knowledge up through my mid-20s, but very little of it was applied towards a meaningful life's purpose. I was too immature to realize the difference between people who grow and live life enthusiastically and people who stagnate and die is often the willingness to be appliers of knowledge.

The term career student is often used to describe people who have a lot of knowledge, but never seem to direct it towards the accomplishment of a worthwhile purpose. Obviously, any successful person is always in school to the extent that the learning process never ends. Yet, without proper application of knowledge to a meaningful life's mission, is education really worth anything?

Eventually, a typist must get on the keyboard. A swimmer must jump in the water. A driver must get behind the wheel. Book learning is only useful up to a point. As Herbert Armstrong, founder of Armstrong College, once said: "Knowledge without action is of no value."

The application of knowledge requires a certain degree of specialization. There's simply too much knowledge for one person to learn in a lifetime. That's why it's so important to understand the vital link between knowledge and purpose. Clearly, one's purpose in life determines what specialized knowledge will be needed.

In short, the shotgun approach to learning is fine up to a point. That's why high school and early college students study a variety of subjects. They're in the accumulation and understanding modes of learning. Ultimately, the rifle approach to learning must be used if application of specific knowledge is the desired target. As a result, colleges offer major fields of study and graduate work to advanced students.

In summary, the key steps of knowledge are:

Awareness → Process → Repetition → Purpose → Application

30

Focus Versus Facts

"Absolute concentration (is) full deployment of one's self."

— *Warren Bennis*
On Becoming A Leader

■　■　■

Concentration, or the ability to focus, is what enables us to make wise use of what we already know. Hence, I believe focus is more important than facts.

I learned about focus the hard way on May 1, 1983—the date of the second annual Chattahoochee Road Runners 10,000 kilometer (6.2 miles) race in Atlanta along the banks of the Chattahoochee River. Our sponsor that year was Coca-Cola thanks to Mike Daly, a club charter member and a manager with this soft drink giant.

As we promoted our road race for weeks in advance, a new Coca-Cola product—diet Coke—was prominently displayed on our race applications and T-shirts, and stressed throughout our advertising campaign. We had the diet Coke logo on everything. There was no doubt who our sponsor was.

On race morning—May 1, 1983—it was my duty as president to greet some 1,200 runners at the starting line. "Welcome to the second annual Chattahoochee Road Runners 10K," I began from a raised platform. "We're delighted with such a large turnout and we're especially grateful to our sponsor . . . Diet Pepsi!"

Those 1,200 runners howled and jeered. Unfortunately, I had no idea what I'd said . . . until I sensed someone approaching me from the rear. It was Mike Daly, the Coca-Cola manager who had arranged the race sponsorship. He bellowed into my ear, "It's diet Coke, idiot!" (Actually, Mike used a stronger word than idiot, but I dare not print it here.)

Oh, I was so embarrassed. I had the facts. I KNEW diet Coke was our sponsor. However, I didn't make wise use of this knowledge because I wasn't focused. I failed to concentrate on that fateful day in 1983 and I learned a valuable lesson. Indeed, focus is more important than facts.

Today, I often use that valuable story to open my seminars. I urge seminar attendees to concentrate, to focus, on how they'll apply what they learn in a meaningful way. After all, knowledge and training are useless without proper application.

Truly, the wise use of knowledge requires crystal clear focus.

31

Becoming an Expert

"How long does it take to attain mastery of a field? A minimum of 10 years."

— *Dr. B. Eugene Griessman*
The Achievement Factors

■ ■ ■

After I'd been in the automobile sales profession for about a year, I thought I knew it all. My income had soared and so had my confidence. Actually, I'd become rather cocky. That all changed one evening when I had the good fortune of doing business with Jim Porterfield.

Jim took delivery of a new automobile. He called a couple of days later and said, "Dick, you obviously have a lot of talent because you sold me a car. But I wonder how much better you'd be with some formal sales training? I represent a company called Sales Training, Inc. and I'd like to talk to you about the work we do. Would Wednesday morning or Thursday evening be more convenient for us to get together and talk about how you can fully develop your sales potential?"

I fought Jim all the way. I didn't want to spend the $1,100 tuition for his five-month course. I didn't want to take that much time out of my busy schedule. I didn't need his course because I was already doing very well. Jim Porterfield countered all my objections and, that's right, I bought.

Well, I finished No. 1 in my class with a 98.4 grade average. My sales and income improved dramatically. More importantly, I learned a valuable lesson. Prior to taking the STI course, I'd never thought of sales as a profession, which Webster's defines as "a calling requiring specialized knowledge and often long and intensive academic preparation."

After completing the course, I realized how little I knew about the sales profession. Just as a mechanic must have the right tools and be able to use them properly, I decided to acquire the right tools for my trade as well. In short, I vowed to pursue the art of mastery.

I began to read every book and article on sales I could find. I began to listen to inspirational and educational tapes. I began to attend seminars and conventions. I began to seek out older, wiser salespeople for their advice. I was on the path to becoming an expert. Incidentally, an expert doesn't have to know everything about their specialty; they just have to know more than the people they're talking to, and that requires ongoing education.

When I moved to the leasing side of the automobile business in 1977, I retained the same zeal for learning. I began to write articles on leasing. I joined the National Vehicle Leasing Association. I started my own leasing company in 1982. I began publishing a newsletter, LEASING LOGIC, a year later. In 1986, I joined the National Speakers Association. By 1987, I was conducting leasing seminars—exactly 10 years after I launched my leasing career!

Today, my seminar clients include many automobile manufacturers, dealerships, associations and financial institutions. I don't say this to boast, but merely to stress it took a decade of hard work and study to become an "overnight success" as an expert in my field.

32

Preparation Versus Luck

"Lucky is what others will call you after your hard work produces results."

— *Og Mandino*
University Of Success

■ ■ ■

I want to share with you how I "lucked" into becoming a professional speaker and trainer.

In 1985, I spent several months researching and writing an article entitled, "The Road To True Success And Happiness." As the theme unfolded, I began to think about turning this article into a book. I wrote a few chapters, but I wasn't happy with the results. I began to think about other uses for this idea. Why not a speech?

As a writer, I felt confident I could turn an article into a speech. What I didn't feel confident in was my speaking skills. In early 1986, I happened to mention my article/speech idea to Ken and Peg Watkins as we had lunch after church. I told them of my desire to speak, of my need to polish my platform skills.

Peg said she knew a lady named Deanna Berg, who was a member of the National Speakers Association (NSA) and its local affiliate, the Georgia Speakers Association (GSA). Deanna mailed me the membership applications and I joined NSA/GSA in March, 1986. I began to attend the monthly meetings of GSA and the conventions of NSA. I began to deliver my speech part-time to civic clubs and other non-profit groups while continuing to earn a full-time living through my automobile leasing company.

At the NSA winter workshop in Atlanta in February, 1987, I met Linda Miles. Based in Virginia Beach, Virginia, Linda has developed a niche within the dental profession. When she asked about my speaking expertise, I told her I gave inspirational speeches for free or little fee. As she looked at my business card, Linda asked a simple question that would change my business dramatically: "Why don't you develop a speaking niche within the automobile leasing industry and get paid as an expert?"

During the next few months, I assembled ideas for lease training seminars. I thought about how I could market this side of my business. While attending a Board of Directors meeting of the Georgia chapter of the National Vehicle Leasing Association in October, 1987, Dave Dunaway, one of the directors, posed the idea of offering a leasing seminar to our members as a fund raiser. Since I'd given an inspirational talk to our chapter a few weeks earlier, the Board asked me if I could deliver a leasing seminar on November 10, 1987. I did and I've been conducting paid leasing seminars ever since.

Was it luck I happened to go to lunch with the Watkins that Sunday afternoon? Was it luck I sat next to Linda Miles at that NSA convention? Was it luck I happened to be at that NVLA Board of Directors meeting? Perhaps. However, it wasn't luck that prepared me to take full advantage of those opportunities. It was years of hard work and dedication, which no amount of luck can offset.

33

Vision

"A mission statement comes from the head; a vision comes from the heart."

— *James J. Mapes*

■ ■ ■

When Dr. Martin Luther King, Jr. delivered his famous "I have a dream" speech, he was speaking from the heart. King probably had no idea what long-range impact his words would have on human relations. Yet, his vision was incredibly clear and he certainly seized a golden opportunity in Washington, D.C. in 1963.

It's important to understand there's a major difference between vision and purpose (or mission). A mission statement is a reflection of one's purpose in life. It's generally a well-defined, realistic statement of what a person wants to be. For example, a mission statement might say, "I want to be an elementary school teacher so I can help children develop good study habits in their formative years."

On the other hand, a vision statement is broader and tends to be more idealistic than a mission statement. King's "I have a dream" speech is a splendid example. An elementary school teacher's vision might read, "I see a day when all children will value their textbooks more than their television sets." It conveys the dream, not the details. The challenge lies in learning to free ourselves from ordinary dreams and visions.

People with vision see possibilities, not impossibilities. People with vision see beyond the problems of the day to the solutions of tomorrow. People with vision believe dreams do come true. As Dr. Benjamin Mays says, "It isn't a calamity to die with dreams unfulfilled, but it is a calamity not to dream."

As an automobile lease trainer, my mission is "to provide lessors with the ethical foundation necessary to gain the trust and respect of their customers and peers; to provide the basic knowledge needed to educate customers in the most professional manner possible; and to provide the inspiration required to gain new customers and increase repeat business and referrals." I'm currently hard at work on that mission.

However, my vision is quite different. I see a day when the image of the automobile industry will be reversed. American consumers will not only love their automobiles, but they'll also love the place and manner in which they are acquired. While that day is not here yet, I'm confident I'll see my vision fulfilled during my lifetime.

Of course, Martin Luther King, Jr. didn't live to see his vision come true. He was gunned down at a Memphis motel in 1968. Nevertheless, he planted the seeds for the sweeping changes that have followed his death. More importantly, many of those who shared King's vision are still struggling to bring his dream to a more vivid reality.

What is your vision? Are you sharing it with others? Don't be afraid to dream. Most greatness has its origin in the hearts of those intrepid dreamers who envisioned a better world, then toiled to make it happen. Truly, our vision helps shape who we are and the impact we'll have on future generations.

34

Goals

"Goals are as essential to success as air is to life."
— *Dr. David Schwartz*
The Magic Of Thinking Big

■ ■ ■

Despite the obvious importance of goal-setting, try walking up to anyone at random and asking if their short-term and long-term goals are in writing. It's a rare person who has completed such a list. Alas, many people just forge ahead in hopes of reaching an eventual destination.

Would a contractor erect a building without a set of blueprints? Would a chef be successful without a proven set of recipes? Would an airline pilot take off without a flight plan? Of course not, yet people often set sail on the journey of life without a worthwhile purpose and corresponding goals.

Could it be that people simply don't set goals because they don't have a simple system to follow in this important planning function? Goal-setting is merely the procedure a person uses to decide where they want to go with what they know. The following seven Rs of goal-setting is a system for your consideration:

> ▸ *Respectable*—If a goal isn't worthwhile, why set it in the first place? Respectable goals can only be established after a worthwhile purpose has been written in the form of a mission statement.

- ▸ *Realistic*—Contrary to popular belief, each and every goal cannot always be achieved. Therefore, set high goals tempered with reality and patience.

- ▸ *Record*—Put goals in writing. Read them often as a vivid reminder for their attainment.

- ▸ *Reduce to the Specific*—Don't say, "I want to move up in the company." Instead, be specific and say, "I'd like to be vice president of marketing by the year ___." It's easier to pursue a pinpointed goal.

- ▸ *Reflect Upon Often*—Constantly visualize the attainment of a goal. It will provide the positive reinforcement necessary to stay focused on the objective.

- ▸ *Relentlessly Pursue*—There are no substitutes for hard work and persistence. As long as a goal is respectable and realistic, keep at it.

- ▸ *Responsibility*—Sometimes the achievement of a particular goal is not possible at a certain point in time. Don't blame others if a goal is not achieved. Simply take personal responsibility by reassessing the importance of a certain goal, then get on with the achievement of other objectives.

35

Priorities

". . . a priority is something which we give precedence
by assigning a degree of urgency or importance to it."
— Patrick M. Morley
The Man In The Mirror

■ ■ ■

In chapter 22, I stressed the importance of a written
personal mission (or purpose) statement. I also said such
a written *purpose* would produce a list of *dominant inter-*
ests that create a measure of balance in life.

From my three dominant interests—God/spiritual, others
and personal—I develop *goals* for each one using the seven
Rs method as discussed in Chapter 34. Finally, I strive to
accomplish these goals by establishing a list of *priorities*
on my daily planning calendar.

For example, let's say someone's statement of purpose
reads as follows: "I want to be the best person possible
spiritually, mentally, physically and emotionally." Now,
let's isolate one of the dominant interests within this
statement—the physical side. The next challenge is to set
goals for the achievement of physical fitness.

As a runner, I set goals each year by determining my
annual mileage (at least 1,000 miles per year since 1980)
and by selecting certain road races I want to run. Since
1978, I've run every Peachtree Road Race on July 4 in
Atlanta, an event that draws 45,000 participants. The real

challenge comes in establishing weekly and daily priorities, including time to do my training runs.

In this particular example, the process looks like this:

Purpose →	Dominant → Interests	Goals →	Priorities
Be the best person possible spiritually, mentally, physically and emotionally.	Physical Fitness (Only one is listed here for demonstration purposes.)	Annual Mileage Road Races	Do four or five training runs each week.

Priorities enable us to pursue our goals by developing a system of daily and weekly activities within the available hours. Here are my five Ds for establishing priorities:

▸ *Determine the Importance*—Make sure a priority is really a priority. Otherwise, it's easy to be busy but unproductive.

▸ *Deadline It*—In listing priorities, arrange them in the order of importance. Assign a day and time on a planning calendar. A deadline creates a sense of urgency, which is essential for the prompt completion of any activity.

▸ *Decide on a Plan of Implementation*—Once it becomes a priority and a deadline is set, decide on the best way to get the job done. **Caution**: Do not over-plan or "paralysis from analysis" is likely.

▸ *Delegate if Possible*—My speaker friend Patricia Fripp says, "There's no point doing well that which you shouldn't be doing at all." Nevertheless, no matter how much work is delegated, the ultimate responsibility belongs to the delegator.

▸ *Do It*—Act on today's priorities because there will be other priorities the next day. National sales trainer Tom Hopkins uses this motto: "I must do the most productive thing possible at every given moment."

36

Attitude

" . . . positive attitude can do more than change some-one's attitude from bad to good. It can change a life."
— *Morris Goodman*
The Miracle Man

■ ■ ■

When I left journalism in 1970 to pursue a career in automobile sales, America was in an era of economic prosperity. I did very well as a salesman for four years. I was offered a job as a dealership sales manager in January, 1974. I didn't think things could get any better and my attitude reflected such euphoria.

Suddenly, the oil crisis hit and business began to deteriorate. Sales plunged dramatically and so did my income and attitude. By August, 1974, I decided to accept a sales position with Aetna Life & Casualty. Still, I continued to be very concerned about the economy.

I happened to read two books that took my attitude to a frightening low—*How To Prepare For The Coming Crash* (Preston) and *You Can Profit From A Monetary Crisis* (Browne). Fortunately, I was also subscribing to *The Kiplinger Letter*, a positive publication in circulation since 1923. On September 26, 1974, I wrote a letter to Austin H. Kiplinger, editor-in-chief.

In part, my letter said: "Do you, with all your experience and available inside information, feel another depression is

close at hand? Can you offer some sound, logical advice
which might help me understand what's going on in the
country economically?"

I received a letter dated October 7, 1974 from Milton
Christie, one of Mr. Kiplinger's senior editors. In part, he
said: "We have read the two books you mentioned. They
are both dooms-saying books that pay no attention to the
basic strength of this country, which is its productive
capacity and the basic financial stability of institutions such
as the one you work for."

The letter continued: " . . . we have seen such books . . .
come and go in the past. When they happen to coincide
with difficult economic periods, they make a big splash. At
other times, they cause hardly a ripple. We . . . are basically
optimistic about the future of our country."

Those encouraging words caused my attitude to make
a 180 degree turn. I spent two successful years with
Aetna—I made the Million Dollar Round Table (MDRT)
in my second year and attended the 1976 MDRT convention in Boston—before deciding to return to the automobile
industry as a leasing manager.

That experience taught me why we become—good or
bad—what we think about, and why attitude is so critical
to our success. In truth, I let the economy, which was
beyond my control, get the best of my attitude, which only
I can control. While I single-handedly couldn't reverse the
economy, I could change how I viewed a tough market.

Clearly, attitude is a choice. We can choose to have a
positive or negative attitude. But believe this—a negative
attitude will not produce positive behavior! Interestingly,
position is a synonym for attitude. Is your attitude in the
right position?

37

Attitude Versus Ability

"I don't care how positive I became, I could not whip the heavyweight champion of the world."

— *Zig Ziglar*
Zig Ziglar's Secrets Of Closing The Sale

■ ■ ■

There is no substitute for ability. Nevertheless, I believe a person's skills are unlikely to reach their full potential without a positive attitude. I also believe a self-confident attitude is often the difference in securing an opportunity to *use* one's ability.

Years ago, I left a job as a sports writer for *The Atlanta Constitution* to enter the Marine Corps. When my four-year enlistment ended, I returned to the *Constitution* to reclaim my former position. I was told that there were no openings, but to check upstairs with the Associated Press (AP).

As I got off the elevator, I noticed a crowd of people glaring at me. I had to elbow my way past this throng into a newsroom filled with noisy teletype machines and desks for about 30 people. Oddly enough, there were only four people in the entire place.

I approached a man named Lamar Matthews, who happened to be the news editor. I told him I'd been a *Constitution* sports writer fours years ago prior to my Marine duty. "Son," Mr. Matthews said, "do you know who those people are out by the elevators?" I didn't. He replied,

"That's our striking writers and teletype operators!" With all the confidence I could muster, I declared: "Mr. Matthews, it must be my lucky day."

Mr. Matthews must have liked my self-confidence because he said, "Biggs, we do need someone to cover the Atlanta Hawks game tonight. Now, you've been away for four years, so just go out there and take some notes. Come back here and we'll help you write your story." Fortunately, I knew something Mr. Matthews didn't know. There was no way they were going to write my story.

The Hawks won at the buzzer in a lengthy game. It was now just five minutes before the copy deadline. There was no way to make it back to the newsroom. I called Mr. Matthews, who seemed a bit concerned. I calmly asked, "Are you sitting at a typewriter, sir?" He was and I replied, "Start typing!" I dictated some quick paragraphs from my notes, beat the deadline and headed back to the AP office.

Mr. Matthews and the others were shaking their heads when I walked into the newsroom. "We don't understand how a rookie could do such a professional job after a four-year absence," said Mr. Matthews. But remember, I knew something that they didn't know.

I explained that I'd been on embassy duty for the past two years in Europe. I had a lot of spare time. I went to the embassy library and read the great American sports writers. I even had the audacity to rewrite their columns. I'd visualize myself covering the action. I'd write lead paragraphs for practice.

Obviously, Mr. Matthews had underestimated my ability. However, I'm convinced my self-confident attitude, more so than my ability, was what led that AP editor to provide such a gracious opportunity to a "rookie" on that winter night in Georgia.

38

Problems:
A State of Mind

---

*"It's not what you don't understand that's the problem;
it's what you understand and don't act upon that's the
problem."*

— *Rev. Burrell Dinkins*
Asbury (KY) Theological Seminar

■ ■ ■

NEWS BULLETIN: Problems are a part of life! The
key question is: Will we solve our problems or complain
about them? Clearly, the difference between solving
problems and complaining about them is essentially a
matter of attitude.

Successful people usually have just as many problems
as anyone else. The difference? Successful people learn to
become professional problem-solvers. On the other hand,
failures tend to develop what Zig Ziglar calls "hardening
of the attitudes." It's a deadly, contagious disease that can
infect anyone who isn't properly protected. The best
protection is a state of mind that refuses to let problems
become one's master.

One of the most masterful problem-solvers I know is C.
Richard Weylman, a dynamic speaker and a close friend.
Since his boyhood days, Richard has been solving some
difficult problems. His mother died when he was five; his

father passed away when he was six. Richard, along with his brother and sister, were split up. He lived in numerous foster homes until 18, then joined the Navy.

During his military service, Richard took a part-time job selling cookware door to door. "It was great training for direct sales," says Richard. "When they told me I'd have to go into a lot of strangers' homes, I certainly didn't have any problem identifying with that." After his military discharge, Richard continued to overcome problems most people would run from—selling industrial laundry supplies business to business; selling Porsches and Audis at a rural dealership where he was the top salesman for 22 consecutive months; and selling a large volume of Rolls Royces at a little dealership in upstate New York primarily by telephone to clients across the nation.

Those experiences led to the launching of a specialty automotive magazine. In the first year, sales topped $1.9 million. Within four years, 118 salespeople sold advertising out of 23 offices. As Vice President of Sales & Marketing, Richard was in the process of establishing a national franchise network when his business partner sold $287,000 in company assets and split. Richard found himself with the pressing problems of no company and no job.

In the summer of 1983, Richard launched his speaking business in his home with a princess telephone on the kitchen counter, a telephone book and no money. He convinced an AT&T manager to go to lunch, which led to his first speaking engagement in Las Vegas. Richard attended the 1983 annual convention of the National Speakers Association in San Francisco "on my last dime so I could learn from the pros." In his first year, he delivered 23 talks and earned a modest $23,000.

Today, Richard is president of The Achievement Group, an Atlanta-based company specializing in niche marketing primarily for the financial services, direct sales and franchise industries. His video learning system, "How To Effectively Target Market And Increase Commissions," is in great demand. He publishes a newsletter entitled *Smart Marketing*. And he speaks about 125 times per year.

Why is he so successful? Richard has the uncanny ability to focus on a client's problems and solve them. He's a master salesman and marketing genius. "I believe you have to make it happen," advises Richard, "not let it happen." Most importantly, Richard realizes his knack for problem-solving isn't all his doing. He's a deeply religious man ("God has really blessed us") and a loyal husband to Jackie, who is also his office manager ("I couldn't have done it without her.").

39

Adversity:
A State of Mind

"Fire is the test of gold; adversity, of strong men."
                    — *Seneca (8 B.C. - 65 A.D.)*

■ ■ ■

I met Clebe McClary at the 1988 annual convention of the National Speakers Association in Phoenix. Make that former Lieutenant Clebe McClary, United States Marine Corps, 1st Recon Platoon, 1967-68, Vietnam. If anyone has the right to have a bad attitude, it's Clebe.

On March 3, 1968, while on patrol in the Quan Duc Valley about 30 miles south of DaNang, 10 of Clebe's 13-man platoon were wounded or killed. Clebe suffered the loss of one eye, his left arm and subsequently underwent 33 operations to retain the use of the rest of his body.

He is a walking miracle. His book, *Living Proof*, is a stirring testament to that fact. But don't feel sorry for this truly special man. Clebe's accomplishments since his injuries are amazing—a tribute to his incredibly enthusiastic attitude in overcoming adversity.

Clebe has run a marathon in three hours and six minutes—just over a seven-minute per mile pace for 26.2 miles! He stayed on the Balke treadmill at Dr. Ken Cooper's Aerobic Center in Dallas for 36 minutes, 36 seconds, a record for the 40-44 age group. He plays tennis, has been a state chairman for the South Carolina Special Olympics and speaks to groups across the nation, including National Football League teams.

Of his many combat awards, his favorite is a plaque he received from the men in his platoon. Taken from a phrase used by his coach at Erskine College, it reads: "In this world of give and take, there are not enough people who are willing to give what it takes."

Unquestionably, Clebe McClary has what it takes to overcome adversity after adversity. While he likes to give the credit to God and his beautiful family—wife Deanna and daughters Tara and Christa—there's no denying his remarkable attitude has played a vital role in his extra-ordinary achievements.

To gain insight into Clebe's attitude in dealing with adversity, listen to what he says in the final chapter of his book: "If God can use a shot-up, one-armed Marine like me, think what he could do for others. He is a God of miracles; I'm living proof." Clebe, from one former Marine to another, I salute your remarkable attitude in overcoming adversity. You're a winner!

40

Failure:
A State of Mind

"Success is going from failure to failure without loss of enthusiasm."

— *Sir Winston Churchill*

■ ■ ■

I'm a two-time college dropout. That's not a goal I remember setting—it just happened. I'm certainly not proud of this fact, and I'm sure some people would consider my academic shortcoming a dismal failure.

When I graduated from high school in 1963, I went to college because, well, it seemed like the thing to do. After all, my grades were good, I enjoyed learning and I was a student leader. I enrolled at the University of South Carolina in Columbia. I joined the band, served as a sports writer for the school newspaper and worked part-time as a waiter.

Things looked wonderful until I received my first semester grades. I did well in one class, barely passed three others and flunked one course. A month into the second semester, I quit. I could have blamed my departure on a shortage of funds, too many extracurricular activities, the divorce of my parents a few months earlier or homesickness.

In retrospect, I simply wasn't mature enough for the challenge of college. During the next few months, I worked as a sports writing intern for *The Atlanta Constitution*. I took a hitchhiking tour of the eastern United States with Pete Jaynes, my boyhood friend, before we joined the Marine Corps in October, 1964.

After my military discharge, I went to work as a writer for the Associated Press in the evenings. I attended Georgia State University in the mornings. Again, I dropped out of college after one semester. I could have placed the blame on working full-time or too little time for studying. The reality was I had other dominant interests such as having fun and dating.

For a long time, I viewed not having a college degree as a major failure in my life. Certainly, my lack of education has cost me some job opportunities. Frankly, I'll admit it would be gratifying to have that certificate framed on my office wall. But as I've matured over the years, I've realized my "educational failure" opened the doors to journalistic experiences at the newspaper and wire service, travel and four adventurous years in the Marine Corps.

The lesson is obvious. There's a fine line between success and failure. In truth, both sides are necessary for us to learn and grow. Instead of saying, "Why me?" when failure occurs, why not say, "How now?" Self pity is the negative side of failure. The positive side is a stronger determination to succeed by learning from our failures.

Have you ever been afraid to fail? Don't be. After all, as Thomas J. Watson, the founder of IBM, once said: "Success is on the far side of failure."

Failure: A State of Mind

41

Inspiration Versus Motivation

"Motivate others by suggestion. Motivate yourself by self-suggestion."
> — *Napoleon Hill & W. Clement Stone*
> Success Through A Positive Mental Attitude

■ ■ ■

Inspiration and motivation appear to be synonymous, but there is a major difference between the two words.

Inspiration is "any stimulus to creative thought." On the other hand, motivation is "some inner drive, impulse or intention that causes a person to do something or act in a certain way." In short, inspiration affects one's *thinking*; motivation influences one's *behavior*.

When I'm asked to give a motivational speech, I politely decline. However, I will give an inspirational speech. As an inspirational speaker, my purpose is not to change the behavior of an audience. Rather, my intent is to stimulate the thinking of an audience. I suppose it could be called indirect motivation.

After all, a person willing to change their thinking can change their behavior through self-motivation. The speaker (or any other inspirer) merely provides the spark for behavioral change. Only the individual listening can make it happen. The one exception, of course, is motivation through force or fear.

When I enlisted in the Marine Corps in 1964, I journeyed to Parris Island, South Carolina for boot camp training. We were greeted late one October evening by a drill instructor (DI) who stood about 6'2", 230. He had a thick neck, a crew cut topped by a "smokey bear" hat and a deep, gravelly voice. He would be our motivator for the next 12 weeks.

"Listen up, sweethearts," he bellowed. "I can't believe they sent such a scuzzy bunch of civilians for me to try and make Marines out of in three months. Why, you look like a herd of sheep milling around out there. But I'll tell you one thing, scumbags. You'd better give your souls to God because the rest of you's mine." (Actually, the wording was considerably harsher, but I'll leave that to your imagination.)

Needless to say, that DI—along with three others—motivated our platoon primarily through force and fear. Considering we were mostly teenagers preparing for the possibility of combat, it's likely force and fear were necessary to motivate us. Besides, I couldn't leave that swamp-infested island and live to tell about it. I had no choice but to be motivated.

But in the business world, it's highly unlikely anyone will tolerate an owner or manager trying to motivate like a Marine DI. As adults, we must be self-motivated while drawing strength from a carefully chosen group of inspirers. It's my wish that the poem in Chapter 42 will inspire you to a greater level of self-motivation.

Inspiration Versus Motivation

42

Self-Motivation

". . . the person who knows how to be motivated doesn't need any cheering section. He has motivation built in."

— *Charlie "Tremendous" Jones*
Life Is Tremendous

■ ■ ■

SELF-MOTIVATION
by Dick Biggs

They say motivation is dead
It's no longer in demand.
Forget the message of passion
We've had all we can stand.

It's the age of information
So please stick to the facts.
Don't bore me with platitudes
It's education that attracts.

To that, I say nonsense!
Give me emotions and desires.
If you want maximum achievement
Then strike motivational fires.

You can go far with knowledge
But the journey is incomplete.
Without a measure of feeling
The trip is bittersweet.

The spark comes from within
It's your internal drive.
Call it self-motivation
That says, "World, I'm alive!"

Look outside for inspiration
For this stimulates thought.
Turn thoughts into action
Or ideas are for naught.

Motivation deals with behavior
Which only you can control.
Take charge of your habits
And master your chosen role.

A worthwhile mission is power
That comes from the inside out.
Others call it enthusiasm
Self-motivation, without a doubt.

43

Desire

"Desire: The starting point of all achievement."
— *Napoleon Hill*
Think And Grow Rich

■ ■ ■

One thing that can't be taught is desire. The fire of desire must be lit from within. Bill Barnes, a friend and customer, has such an internal fire.

Bill's intense desire, coupled with that of partner Tony Hobson, led to the formation of Hobson, Barnes & Associates, Inc. in 1982. HBA is a marketing services company based in Atlanta. They've worked hard to develop an impressive list of clients.

On June 21, 1991, Bill Barnes, 48 years young, suffered a massive stroke. It left his right side paralyzed. He couldn't walk, talk, tie his shoes or do any of the hundreds of things we take for granted each day. Fortunately, Bill's desire has sparked an amazing comeback.

Five months after his stroke, Bill was walking. He was talking—slowly but understandably. He was even driving his automobile, an ordeal that required passing a rigid four-hour test to regain his driver's license. He saw all of these challenges as a "competition with nature."

"I've come a long way since the hospital gave me a speech test and I answered every question all wrong," says Bill. He attended an intensive 12-week language course at the University of Michigan "to fine tune my speech. If I die tomorrow, I'll die trying to perfect my speech," promises Bill. That's desire.

Bill attributes much of his recovery to Cathy Williams, a hospital physical therapist. "She understands my desire," Bill suggests. "She has made a difference. I would not accept that I couldn't walk. I'm sure of the fact of positive thinking."

As a part of his physical therapy, Bill placed photographs of his friends on a wall. "I wanted to have as much going for me as I could," Bill said. "The photos were my mental support." He even had Hobson, Barnes & Associates T-shirts printed with the words "We Can Do It Together" on the front and "Bill Barnes Comeback Tour" on the back. He even joked that the title of his book should be *Never Play Checkers With A Man Who Has Just Had A Stroke*.

Perhaps Bill's desire is best reflected by the skiing analogy Cathy Williams used throughout his physical therapy. "Bill," she said, "you can come down the hill easy or you can come down schussing."

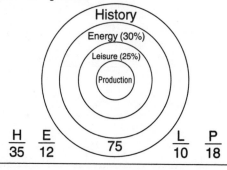

44

Procrastination

"Time is life. It is irreversible and irreplaceable. To waste your time is to waste your life, but to master your time is to master your life and make the most of it."
— *Alan Lakein*
How To Get Control Of Your Time And Life

■ ■ ■

Procrastination is perhaps the most deadly word in the English language. It's the worst nightmare of decisiveness and public enemy No. 1 of achievement. Life is often squandered away due to these six words: "I will get around to it."

Rather than dwell on the many reasons why people procrastinate, let's examine the folly of not acting. The following chart assumes the average person will live for 75 years. Within the rings, the letters H-E-L-P stand for history, energy, leisure and production. Consider these facts for a 35-year-old person:

History stands for the 35 years this person has lived. Those years are gone forever, but there's still 40 years left IF the average life span of 75 is attained.

If a person is to maintain their energy level, let's say an average of seven hours of sleep per day is required. That's about 30% of a person's day or 12 years of the remaining 40.

But wait! Most people will spend about 25% of those 40 remaining years enjoying leisure activities with their family and friends. That's another 10 years, so what is really left? Only 18 productive years for a 35-year-old person IF they live to the average age of 75 (75 − 35 = 40 − 12 = 28 − 10 = 18). It simply doesn't make any sense to waste valuable time when life is so fleeting.

Quite often, procrastination is a weak excuse that becomes a believable reason for half-stepping through life. The procrastinator spends a lifetime in the twilight zone between thinking and doing. At life's end, the saddest words of all are often spoken by the procrastinator: "If I only had it to do over again."

Obviously, there are times when action must be delayed. But to habitually procrastinate is a dangerous addiction. There is rarely a perfect time to do anything. Act as soon as you can and try not to second guess your decisions.

45

Decision-Making

"The difficulty in life is the choice."
— *George Moore*
The Bending Of The Bough

■ ■ ■

The opposite of procrastination is action, which generally requires making some difficult choices. I recall such a decision-making dilemma one winter afternoon.

It doesn't snow often in Atlanta. However, this northwest Georgia metropolis is virtually paralyzed for several days when it does snow. We simply don't have enough snow removal equipment and most people aren't prepared to drive in such hazardous conditions.

On January 13, 1982, the snow began to fall heavily about 3 p.m. I was at work and we were told to go home. As I drove out the rear entrance, I quickly discovered the heavy traffic was moving at a snail's pace. It took an hour to go about a mile as cars were sliding all over the road and into each other.

I had to make a decision. Do I continue to inch along, risk damage to me and my car and, if I'm fortunate, get home several hours later? Or, is there something I can do to change the situation? It occurred to me that my running clothes were in the car trunk. I was about six miles from home. I pulled into an apartment complex parking lot, changed clothes in the car and set out for home at a leisurely pace.

It proved to be a wise decision. Cars and people were stranded all over the highway. I was able to keep a slow, steady pace as the snow continued to fall. People were offering all sorts of encouragement. I even stopped a few times to help stranded motorists push their cars back on to the highway.

Some 90 minutes later, I arrived home safely and turned on the news. The entire city was trapped. It took some people 10 hours to get home. Many others ended up at motels and restaurants. It was the worst snow storm to hit Atlanta in many years.

That was also the same day Air Florida flight 90 hit the 14th Street Bridge in Washington, D.C. Seventy-eight people died in that disaster. Those people didn't have any choice in that tragic crash because it was out of their control. Once in the Potomac River, a few people were rescued from those frigid waters. As I heard that awful news, I was happy I'd decided to take control of what was a difficult but not impossible situation.

When I made my decision to run home that snowy afternoon, I realized it was somewhat risky. There was also a risk of driving in the snow. I chose what seemed like the least perilous risk. Fortunately, a difficult choice resulted in a favorable outcome.

When faced with a tough decision, give careful consideration to the facts at hand. Make a decision. Act with the knowledge you'll probably make more good choices than bad ones over a lifetime. Remember, your success or failure will depend upon the choices you make each day of your life. Anticipate success, but don't be afraid to fail.

46

Sense of Humor

"Humor is indeed the balancing pole that keeps us on the tightrope of life."

— *Russ Fisher*
In Search Of The Funny Bone

■ ■ ■

I have a lot of humorist friends in the National Speakers Association. They have an uncanny ability to express real life observations in a very funny way. Why are they so humorous? The most common answer is, "I just *think* funny."

While some people seem to have a natural inclination to think funny, I believe a sense of humor is something each of us can develop. After all, life has enough difficult and serious moments. We simply need the lighter side to keep things in perspective. Perhaps the greatest humor of all is learning to laugh at ourselves.

Consequently, I've learned to use funny personal stories when I speak. Chances are, a joke has been heard or it's off-color and inappropriate. If I tell a funny personal story, it will be new to the audience and demonstrate that I can laugh at myself.

Children are a wonderful source of humor. I remember being asked to speak to a group of elementary school kids after I ran the 1981 New York City Marathon. The teacher of this class, Marilyn Donahoo Haney, was one of my high school classmates. She thought her students would enjoy hearing about this famous event.

Now, please understand that I completed this 26.2-mile event in a modest time of three hours, 34 minutes and 44 seconds. I was the 5,643rd finisher out of some 14,500 runners. Obviously, I was a middle-of-the-pack runner. What I didn't know was Marilyn's kids assumed I was an elite runner.

I spoke for about 15 minutes to a class of about 25 fourth-graders. All eyes were fixed upon me. They hung on every word. I was amazed by the polite conduct of these children. As I finished up, I thanked everyone and headed for the door.

Suddenly, a cute little girl raced to my side and exclaimed loudly, "Mr. Biggs, can I have your autograph?" I was stunned. No one had ever requested my autograph. "Of course, you can," I replied, not wanting to hurt her feelings. At once, every kid raced to line up behind this daring girl. Embarrassed but flattered, I signed some 25 autographs. Those kids made my day!

While I'm not certain if those children went home that evening and told their parents they got the autograph of a famous person, I do know that story has been good for a lot of laughs over the years. Indeed, humor is all around us. If you'll develop a keen sense of humor, you'll be a more balanced, happier person.

47

Complacency

"Don't ever think you've got it made in life because complacency can be your downfall."
— *Thelma P. (Hall) Askew*
(My mother)

■ ■ ■

Webster's defines complacency as "self satisfaction accompanied by unawareness of actual dangers or deficiencies." To put it another way, a complacent thinker is a person who is resting on past achievements and so-called security rather than looking for ways to improve in the future.

Since 1970, my livelihood has been derived almost exclusively from commission sales and self-employment income. I've found when I get complacent—and I surely have—my income declines. When I'm busy marketing and promoting, my income eventually goes up.

As a result, I've learned never to get too high on my successes or too low on my setbacks. I've also realized job security is not a paycheck because what happens if a job is lost? True job security is a person's ability and a mind set that never accepts complacency for very long.

My longest period of complacency occurred in the first five months of 1982 when I became quite anxious to start my own business and didn't have the guts to act. Don Voyles, my sales manager at Ed Voyles Oldsmobile in

Atlanta, called me in for a morning talk on May 12. "Dick, you've been in the top 10 salespeople in the Southeastern Region for several years," said Don. "But lately you've been coasting and your sales reflect it. I suggest you get back to your old self real soon."

I went to lunch that day with two of my best friends, Frank Crane and Ron Creasy. "When I return to work," I told them, "I'm resigning. I'm not kidding anyone but myself. I'm not going to do anything until I decide if business ownership is for me." Frank drove me home that afternoon after I turned in my company vehicle. I spent the entire summer pondering my entrepreneurial future.

Fortunately, I had saved some money and was single with minimal expenses. I began to ease my way out of this prolonged complacency. In September, I decided to establish Biggs Automobile Leasing Corp. on a scant $2,000 and a lot of determination. On October 4, 1982, I incorporated the business.

Since that memorable day, I must admit I've flirted with complacency from time to time. That's only natural. But I don't dwell on my past achievements for very long for fear I might have to go back to work for someone else. That very thought tends to keep my complacency to a minimum and my enthusiasm for future growth at its maximum.

48

Resourcefulness

*"When sudden emergencies arise, then of all times you
need a clear mind, calm nerves, rapid thinking, sound
reasoning. You need resourcefulness."*

— *Herbert Armstrong*
The Seven Laws Of Success

■ ■ ■

Resourcefulness is a special attribute that allows us to
keep on keeping on in difficult times. It's the ability to
think practically, to use common sense in a time of crisis.

Resourceful people make the best use of the resources
at hand in spite of unfavorable situations. They have a
knack for overcoming obstacles and seeing a task to its
completion. They have a mental tenacity that says, "I won't
let this situation get the best of me."

In the spring of 1979, I tore the ligaments in my left
foot while playing basketball. I was particularly distressed
when I found out I'd be on crutches for six weeks and
wouldn't be able to run for two months. How would I
handle such a trying time?

Perhaps resourcefulness is born out of necessity. Since
I couldn't run, I began to think about when I'd be able to
run again. I'd run my longest distance ever in 1978 (12.4
miles) at Callaway Gardens, a wooded resort near Colum-
bus, Georgia. I began to think about what it would be like
to run my first marathon—a distance of 26.2 miles!

I began to read all the articles and books on mara-
thoning I could find. I talked with anyone who had run this
grueling distance to learn about training tips. Gradually, I
began to prepare a training schedule for the Callaway
Gardens marathon that November.

When my cast came off in early May, it seemed like an
eternity before two weeks elapsed and my podiatrist gave
me the okay to start back running. I could barely run a mile
that first day but it didn't matter. I was just happy to be
exercising again.

Six months later, I crossed the finish line of my first
marathon at Callaway Gardens. It was a proud moment, but
it probably wouldn't have happened without the lesson I
learned from my injury. When times seem tough, resourcefulness is a great teacher if the student is willing to learn.

49

Reflection

"Take time to confer with yourself and tap your supreme thinking power . . . the successful person in any field takes time to confer with himself."
— *David J. Schwartz*
The Magic Of Thinking Big

■ ■ ■

I once heard CBS commentator Charles Osgood remark, "We can become a hostage to our busyness." Isn't that often true? We get so caught up in our daily routine that we don't spend any quality time in reflection.

One of the things I've done every year since 1974 is spend some time in reflection during the week between Christmas and New Year's. I think about the year that has just passed. I make some notes of all that's happened—good and bad. I also think about the year ahead and what I'd like to be, do and have. Again, I make some notes.

From these thoughts and notes, I write a review of the year. I also list some of my resolutions for the upcoming year. I've found this reflective process helps in two ways. First, it makes me take a candid look at my life for the past year. If I've had a wonderful year, I give thanks to God. If it hasn't been such a good year, I thank God for giving me the strength and courage to persevere.

Second, this year-end reflection makes me look to the future with excitement and anticipation. I try not to make too many resolutions because it's difficult to focus on a large list. Generally, I try to pick only one or two objectives within the three dominant interests of my life.

I'll spend other time in reflection during the year, but this period at year's end is the most crucial. It forces me back to the basics of life—the things that are really important. It's time well spent.

What's really fascinating is to read these reviews years later. Each year is like a piece of a jigsaw puzzle as the big picture of my life develops. Such reflection also makes me realize how quickly the picture will be completed.

What does you life's picture look like? Are you working on a masterpiece or a mishmash? Set aside some time for reflection to improve the quality of your life. You're worth it!

50

Wisdom

"It is characteristic of wisdom not to do desperate things."

— Henry David Thoreau

■ ■ ■

My Grandmother Hall used to tell my mother, "Each stage and age of life brings with it certain benefits." While some people can be incredibly wise beyond their years or terribly unwise in spite of their age, I suppose one of aging's benefits is wisdom.

Wisdom is a combination of qualities such as knowledge, experience and sound judgment. It's an innate sense that makes us think before we act. Wisdom allows us to strike a balance between the work we do and the life we lead.

Wisdom can't be bought and it certainly can't be attained overnight. It comes gradually. If we're very blessed, it remains with us to the end. In truth, wisdom is a collection of what we learn from our successes and failures; from our wise decisions and mistakes; from our risk-taking and cautiousness; and from our opportunities and problems.

This "To Think" section has attempted to identify some of the qualities which afford us the opportunity to become wiser as we grow older. Knowledge, attitude, desire, self-motivation, goals, priorities, a sense of humor, decisiveness and vision are just some of the qualities that enable us to grow, to become better balanced.

The saddest circumstance is to fail to learn from our experiences. Life is so short. We simply don't come into this world with the collective wisdom of previous generations already implanted in our minds and ready to use. Each person must live and learn in their own way.

Fortunately, we don't have to do it alone. We can accelerate our pursuit of wisdom by learning from those with more knowledge, experience and sound judgment. It's what Cavett Robert, the founder of the National Speakers Association, refers to as "OPE—Other Peoples' Experience."

Wisdom enables us to see the big picture. Wisdom says, "This, too, shall pass." Wisdom provides the proper perspective for dealing with life's ups and downs. Most of all, wisdom beckons us to think things through very clearly so that our actions are a reflection of our true intentions.

PART III

"TO DO"

The Physical Force

"The meaning of life is to find value in what we do."
— *Gerhard Gschwandtner*

51

Creeds Versus Deeds

"The world pays more attention to your conduct than it does to your creed."

— *Michael A. Guido, D.D.*

■ ■ ■

There's often a big difference between what a person believes and how one behaves. Frankly, hypocrisy may pose the single greatest threat to achieving a reasonable degree of balance in life.

The word hypocrisy, which comes from the Greek word *hypokrisis* meaning "the act of playing a part," is commonly associated with religion. Since our creeds are often based upon our religious beliefs, it always casts a cloud of insincerity upon religion when our deeds conflict with our creeds. The case of Jim and Tammie Faye Bakker and the PTL scandal of the 1980s is an infamous example.

Thus, it behooves every individual to carefully examine their credos with two questions in mind. Are my core beliefs and values rooted in a firm foundation? Do my daily deeds reflect the high principles of my credo? It's absolutely critical that a person's behavior parallel their beliefs or an unbalanced life is assured. Literally, a hypocritical lifestyle will wear a person out.

Now, I'm not referring to living a perfect life. Jesus Christ was the only one who ever accomplished that feat. But as my friend Rick Page likes to say, "Learn right from wrong; then do right." Our creeds should be the basis for *knowing* the difference between right and wrong. The challenge is in *doing* right in order to live a more fulfilling and harmonious life.

"Practicing what you preach" is indeed a difficult deed. In fact, it may be the single biggest reason why life is so difficult. Nevertheless, life becomes even more complex for the person who chooses to say one thing and do another. Life isn't a stage play in which we act out a role. It's about being real and living out our beliefs to the best of our ability.

A creed is only as good as the deeds that follow. We can't expect our children, friends or fellow employees to listen to our noble words when our conduct is playing a different tune. That which is heard is long forgotten when it differs from what is seen.

In the struggle to achieve consistency between beliefs and behavior, Carl Sewell offers this wise advice in *Customers For Life*: "How would my actions appear if they were described tomorrow on the front page of the local newspaper?"

52

Just Do It

"I've always been haunted by the gap between theory and practice, the difference between what one thinks and teaches and what one does."

— *Warren Bennis*
On Becoming A Leader

■ ■ ■

I've wanted to write a book for a long time. I made half-hearted efforts in the late 1970s and mid-1980s, but somehow I couldn't maintain my focus or drive. Finally, in 1990, the organizational format for this book began to take shape and I began to get excited again.

Prior to going on vacation in August, 1991, I was talking to my friend Dr. Gene Griessman, a speaker and author of *The Achievement Factors*. I remember telling Gene about my book writing frustrations and why it needed to be a more pressing goal if publication was to be achieved. In his straightforward, succinct manner, Gene gave me three simple words of advice: "Just do it!"

While vacationing in Asheville, North Carolina, I planned an 18-week schedule that would produce four chapters per week by the end of 1991. If I could stay on track, I'd have 72 of 100 chapters completed between September and December. I'd be able to see light at the end of the publishing tunnel. On December 31, 1991, I'd completed 68 chapters. I was on the road for the first five

---

months of 1992, but I was able to write the remaining 32 chapters during the summer of 1992.

Basically, Gene's advice was the same as the highly successful advertising campaign conducted by Nike, the sport shoe company. In fact, I have one of those Nike decals prominently displayed in my office—Just Do It! It serves as a vivid reminder to act on my ideas.

What I've discovered about acting on an idea is it creates an enormous amount of energy. The hardest part of any task always seems to be getting started. Once we get going, the power of momentum is an awesome force. I believe that's what Ralph Waldo Emerson had in mind when he said, "Do the thing and you shall have the power."

Truly, action ("do the thing") goes a long way towards giving us the confidence to see a task to its end ("and you shall have the power.") Dreaming, talking and learning will only carry us so far. Eventually, action must be taken if success is to be realized. In a nutshell, we need to "just do it."

In their own way, Warren Bennis, Gene Griessman, Ralph Waldo Emerson and Nike helped me turn the concept of this book into the printed pages before you. There is never enough time to do everything we'd like to do. We simply have to decide what is most important and go after it. Edward Everett Hale understood the power of each individual when he wrote the poem "I Am Only One:"

> I am only one
> But still I am one.
> I cannot do everything
> But still I can do something.
> And because I cannot do everything
> I will not refuse to do the something
> I can do.

53

Physical Fitness Versus Healthiness

"Few Americans are physically fit. Fewer still realize this seemingly obvious fact."
— *John David Cantwell, M.D.*
Stay Young At Heart

■ ■ ■

A physically fit person isn't always a healthy person. Jim Fixx, author of the best-selling *The Complete Book Of Running*, was physically fit. But Fixx wasn't healthy and he died of a heart attack at 52.

About 16 years before his sudden death, Fixx took up running. He worked his way up to 60-70 miles per week. He quit smoking. He dropped 60 pounds down to a trim 170. Fixx became a model of physical fitness. Why, then, wasn't he healthy?

First, Jim Fixx had the No. 1 risk factor of heart disease as identified by the American Heart Association—family history and heredity. His father suffered two heart attacks and the second one killed him at 43. Prior to implementing his rigid running program, Fixx had a sedentary lifestyle, a poor diet, a weight problem, a very high cholesterol count (250) and an addiction to heavy cigarette smoking.

Second, Fixx was under a lot of stress prior to his death. He had been through two divorces, several job changes and a $50,000 investment loss. Due to the fame of his books, Fixx traveled a lot and was in demand for interviews and public speaking—activities he found very stressful.

In *Running Without Fear*, Dr. Ken Cooper of the famed Cooper Clinic in Dallas, explores the death of Fixx. His autopsy revealed the heart of an unhealthy man—severe blockage of his coronary arteries; scar tissue indicating at least three minor heart attacks before the one that killed him; and an abnormally enlarged heart. What else could Fixx have done to be healthier?

Dr. Cooper suggests following these four "Longevity Habits" are critical: "(1) Have regular preventive medical exams, with adequate cardiovascular and cancer screening tests. (2) Eat a low-fat, low-sugar, low-salt, high fiber diet, which will keep your weight within normal limits. (3) Follow a moderate but systematic aerobic exercise program. (4) Avoid tobacco in all forms, but particularly avoid cigarette smoking."

"Just doing one, two, or three won't do the trick," warns Dr. Cooper. "Take Jim Fixx. He did a great job incorporating the last three habits into his daily routine for the last 15 or so years of his life. But he omitted the first—the need for an annual health exam with a stress test. That omission probably led him down the road to sudden death." Ironically, Fixx was at the Cooper Clinic six months before his death and declined a stress test—a test, if properly administered and interpreted, can detect arterial blockage with reasonable accuracy.

It's difficult to do anything when there's no physical energy. Yet, physical fitness alone won't ensure good health and a more productive life. Stress testing can help bridge the gap between physical fitness and good health. Make a vow to follow Dr. Cooper's four practical suggestions. You'll be more productive, happier and healthier. That's not a bad trade-off, is it?

54

Enthusiasm

"Take on enthusiasm and the discouraged and defeat-prone personality is reborn as a positive emotionally-charged dynamo."

— *Robert H. Schuller*
You Can Become The Person You Want To Be

■ ■ ■

Enthusiasm can make the difference between acceptance and rejection. In May, 1984, I witnessed the power of this phenomenon called enthusiasm at the annual convention of the Road Runners Club of America (RRCA) in Michigan City, Indiana.

Less than three years earlier, I had co-founded the Chattahoochee Road Runners (CRR) with Ron Creasy and Ron Varner. We grew from three members to about 150 members in our first three years. We were fairly well known in Georgia, but our club was a virtual unknown on the national running scene.

J. David Murray, our third president, called me in early 1984 with an idea. "Let's attend the RRCA convention this year," said David, "and bid for the convention to be held in Atlanta in 1985." While I admired David's passion for this ambitious goal, I was concerned our club was too small and too new to have a fighting chance.

Apparently, David's enthusiasm fanned my enthusiasm. I agreed to accept his awesome challenge. We knew our competition was two older, more prestigious clubs with 1,000 or more members. If the CRR was to win the bid, we had to be the most prepared, the most enthusiastic.

We spent several weeks working on a detailed written proposal. We assembled a colorful visual display highlighting the sights of Atlanta. We honed our presentation until it was second nature. We couldn't wait to get to Michigan City.

Perhaps to the surprise of all the convention delegates but David and me, the CRR was selected to host the 1985 RRCA convention in Atlanta. How did we do it? I'm convinced we simply wanted this event more than the older, bigger clubs. Our enthusiasm, coupled with meticulous preparation, made the difference. This enthusiasm carried over to our members, who staged what is now referred to as THE convention that changed the way RRCA conventions have been conducted ever since.

Truly, enthusiasm is the driving force behind exceptional achievement. Enthusiasm is the difference between going through the motions and succeeding. Enthusiasm is a quality no effective person can be without. The Greeks called it *enthouslasmos*, which means "to be filled with spirit."

55

Burn Out

"Burn out doesn't stem from too few expectations, but from too many. And over the years, our world— particularly in America—has become a storehouse of expectations."

— *Dr. Herbert J. Freudenberg*
Burn Out

■ ■ ■

Burn out is the extinguishing of a person's spiritual, mental, physical or emotional enthusiasm. Specifically, burn out usually occurs when a single dominant interest becomes our life; or when we overcommit to several dominant interests.

The workaholic is the most common example of a single dominant interest becoming our life. In the early 1980s, I was working too hard at a job that left little time for personal interests. Eventually, I burned out so badly I quit my job and didn't work during the summer of 1982. Ironically, that was one of my most depressing periods and one of my most positive turning points ever.

I learned for a person to burn out, there had to be flame at some point in time. How can someone die if there was never life? My challenge was discovering a way to reignite the fire. Happily, the fire was rekindled in the fall of 1982 when I went into business for myself.

I almost burned out again in the late 1980s after stretching myself too thin among my three dominant interests. Besides running a business, I was a leader in four professional organizations. I was very involved in my church and community. I was committed to an intense physical fitness program. And, of course, I was spending time with my wife, stepdaughters and friends. My circuits were overloaded.

While I wanted the balance of these three dominant interests—God/spiritual, others and self—I was on the verge of burn out from trying to do too much in these areas. I had to make some agonizing decisions. It meant dropping a couple of organizations, scaling back in others, reducing my exercise program and not planning too many social activities.

Since then, I've tried very hard not to let one exclusive interest dominate my life. I've also been rather careful about accepting too many responsibilities within each dominant interest. Striking such a balance isn't easy, but it sure beats burning out.

Frankly, burn out doesn't have to happen. We can maintain our zest for living by carefully monitoring the choices we make about our number of dominant interests and the degree of activities within each one. We can enjoy the ecstasy of burning brightly instead of dealing with the agony of burning out. With the proper balance and variety, life is less stressful and more satisfying.

56

The Habit of Discipline

"Every single qualification of success is acquired through habit. Men form habits and habits form futures. If you do not deliberately form good habits, then unconsciously you will form bad ones."
— *Albert E. N. Gray*
The Common Denominator Of Success

■ ■ ■

Mr. Gray, an executive of the Prudential Insurance Company of America, delivered his famous "The Common Denominator Of Success" speech at the 1940 annual convention of the National Association Of Life Underwriters in Philadelphia. What is that common denominator? "The common denominator of success—the secret of every man who has ever been successful—lies in the fact that he formed the habit of doing things that failures don't like to do."

I first read that speech in 1974 when I went to work for Aetna Life & Casualty. I've carried that pamphlet in my planning calendar all these years because it helped change my life. How? I learned that discipline is the ability to change bad habits into good habits.

For example, we deliberately develop the conscious good habit of setting the alarm clock each night to avoid oversleeping. The bad habit, which requires no conscious act, would be to fail to set the alarm clock. The difference is self-discipline.

Many of our habits—good or bad—are formed in our early years. That's why it's so critical for parents and other adult leaders to teach discipline to children. "By the time we reach adulthood," says Warren Bennis in his book *On Becoming A Leader*, "we are driven as much by habit as by anything else, and there is an infinity of habit in us."

The challenge lies in cultivating our bad habits into good habits. No one will ever eliminate all of their bad habits. The secret is to have more good habits than bad ones, and self-discipline can make that an attainable goal. That's why Mr. Gray's words are as true today as they were more than 50 years ago.

An undisciplined life is a rocky road. An abundance of bad habits can keep a person from reaching their full potential. Conversely, a life filled with self-discipline is a bee line to true success and happiness. It's all a matter of mastering our good habits or being mastered by our bad habits.

In *I Am Your Constant Companion*, the anonymous author says it so well:

> Take me, train me, be firm with me
> And I will place the world at your feet.
> Be easy with me and I will destroy you.
> Who am I?
> I am habit.

57

Time Management

*"The great dividing line between success and failure
can be expressed in five words: 'I did not have time'."*
— *Franklin Field*

■ ■ ■

Since everyone has 24 hours per day, perhaps personal
management might be a more appropriate phrase than time
management. After all, in order to be good time managers,
don't we first have to be good self-managers?

Good self-management includes, among other things, a
balancing of our life's dominant interests. That's part of
what this book is all about. We must first decide *what* we
want to spend our time doing before we can decide *how* the
time will be allotted. If we're spending too much time
doing things we don't want to do, our lives become too
stressful and unbalanced.

Therefore, our dominant interests should be chosen
carefully, then displayed for viewing each week. I keep this
list in the front of my planning calendar. I usually spend
a few minutes every Sunday evening deciding how much
time will be designated in the coming week for the three
dominant interests of my life (see Chapter 22). The activities might change some during the week, but at least I have
a reasonable idea of how my time will be spent.

As simple as it may sound, these two things will make
a dramatic change in a person's life—the *purchasing* of a

planning calendar and the *using* of this time management tool. Yet, many people never buy such a calendar. Worse yet, they acquire one and never use it. A person who does both will never be the same again.

I happen to use Day-Timer's senior pocket size calendar. It fits conveniently in my suit pocket, which is ideal for my travel schedule. I don't use any other backup system at the office or home, so it virtually eliminates any confusion. I write appointments on one side, things to do on the other side. As each activity is accomplished, it's checked off the list. And I don't just write down business activities. I include personal matters such as church, exercise, social outings, errands, etc.

At the end of the day, I'm able to ascertain two important things. First, I can see what I've accomplished. If it has been a very productive day, the feeling of pride is quite satisfying. Second, if I haven't done everything I set out to do—and this happens—I transfer those activities to newly assigned days. Eventually, an activity is a must and gets done or it's no longer important and is dropped.

What are you spending your time doing? Are you organized in such a way to get the maximum out of this remarkable resource called time? Remember, time is life and life is precious. William Hazlitt, in *The Feeling Of Immortality In Youth*, summed up time (or personal) management this way: "As we advance in life, we acquire a keener sense of the value of time. Nothing else, indeed, seems of any consequence, and we become misers in this respect."

58

Seize the Day

In the movie Dead Poets Society, *actor Robin Williams plays an English teacher at a stuffy New England prep school in the 1950s. He constantly challenges his students with the Latin phrase "carpe diem" or "seize the day."*

■ ■ ■

Time cannot be recaptured. Oh, we can look at a photo album or a video with fond memories. We can read a book or newspaper clipping to find out how it once was. But we can never go back in person to that very day because time marches on.

Time cannot be accelerated, either. Sure, we can dream and visualize. We can look forward to an upcoming day with hope and enthusiasm. But no matter how hard we try, we cannot make a day arrive before its time.

Yet, it's quite common to hear people talk about the "good old days" or tell someone how it's going to be "one of these days." Whatever happened to today? In reality, the moment is all we have. Tomorrow is not promised to us. Yesterday is gone forever.

I believe we should learn from history but not dwell on the past. "What's done is done" were the immortal words in Shakespeare's *Macbeth*. I believe we should plan for the future without wishing our lives away. In *Interludes*, Nixon

Waterman said, "We shall do so much in the years to come, but what have we done today?"

Now that I'm middle-aged, I'm more mindful of the true wisdom of "seizing the day" than ever before. The birthday card I received from my mother on my 45th birthday offered this profound advice:

> Look to this day . . .
> for yesterday
> is but a dream,
> and tomorrow
> is only a vision
> . . . but today well-lived
> makes every yesterday
> a dream of happiness
> and every tomorrow
> a vision of hope.
>
> —from the *Sanskrit*

Live today as if there will be no others. Don't waste valuable time lamenting about yesterday's woes or dreading tomorrow's challenges. Be grateful for each day as it comes. Live today to its fullest. If you're fortunate to live at least 75 years, make each one of those nearly 27,400 todays count. In short, "seize the day!"

59

Sense of Urgency

*" . . . the two factors that define an activity are **urgent** and **important**. Urgent means it requires immediate attention. It's 'NOW!' "*

— *Stephen R. Covey*
The Seven Habits Of Highly Effective People

■　■　■

Most of us struggle with the difficult task of balancing what we *need* to do now (urgent) with what we *want* to do over a lifetime (important).

In Chapter 35, I discussed the mental challenge of organizing our priorities to allow for optimal time management. Yet, no matter how well we plan, each day seems to present unplanned urgencies that require our attention immediately. As a result, important matters are often replaced by urgent matters.

My journalistic background provided invaluable training in developing a sense of urgency. There are always important stories that deserve to be published. In fact, every editor usually has a backlog. But when a major, unexpected story unfolds—a war breaks out, a world leader dies, an airplane crashes or an earthquake strikes—the important is replaced by the urgent.

In the early days of my Associated Press career, the Barbara Jane Mackle case broke in Atlanta. Miss Mackle, a student at Emory University and the daughter of a wealthy family, was kidnapped on December 17, 1968 and buried alive. Since the authorities didn't know where she was buried, it became a race against time to find her before she suffocated.

This story became so urgent virtually our entire newsroom staff worked on this case. Stories that normally would have been important seemed insignificant. When Miss Mackle was found unharmed and her kidnappers were arrested, the newsroom was able to refocus on several important stories.

The harsh reality is that life is a constant shuffling of the urgent and the important. We go about our days and weeks doing what we deem important. Suddenly, a parent or spouse dies, a child is in an accident or a friend becomes seriously ill. In such cases, the important is now urgent. In other cases, we concoct urgencies that aren't even important.

It's virtually impossible to plan for the urgent matters of life. What we can do is develop a highly focused sense of urgency to help us deal more efficiently with what has to be done now so that there's more time to concentrate on the important things we want to do later. Otherwise, it's easy to convince ourselves that everything is urgent, leaving little time for the important matters that shape the long-term quality of our lives.

Have you ever considered what is *really* important in life? I think you'll find your list of important lifetime concerns will be a lot shorter than your list of daily urgencies. In pondering the important issues of life, I came up with these three:

1. My belief in God and eternal life.

2. The health and safety of family members, friends and myself.

3. The favorable impact I might have on the lives of those I touch during the short time we're given on this earth.

60

Dare to Risk

"Remember, if you take risks, you may still fail. However, if you don't take risks, you will surely fail. More often than not, the greatest risk of all is to do nothing."
— From a speech by Robert C. Goizueta
Chairman & CEO, The Coca-Cola Company

■ ■ ■

Any risk has the potential for reward or misfortune. Nevertheless, winning or losing isn't nearly as important as the willingness to try, to dare to risk.

I learned about risk-taking as an 18-year-old during the summer of 1964. Pete Jaynes, my boyhood friend, talked me into joining the Marine Corps in June. We signed up for four years on what was known as the 120-day plan. That meant we got to go to boot camp on the buddy system at a slightly higher pay scale. However, we had four months before we had to report to Parris Island, South Carolina.

Meantime, we decided to do some traveling. What started out as a week's vacation in Miami turned into a hitchhiking tour of the eastern United States. For 18 days, we put our trust primarily in people we didn't know and would probably never see again. Talk about risk!

We hitched 42 rides from Miami to Orlando, Columbia, Charlotte, Asheville, Lexington, Cincinnati, Chicago, Indianapolis, Louisville, Nashville, Chattanooga and Atlanta. We never had more than $21 between us. Besides all those rides, people bought us meals, provided lodging and occasionally some cash. A guy named Jack Stewart even let us drive his Buick Electra convertible while he slept in the back seat.

Except for a couple of minor incidents, we experienced a safe, exciting and memorable adventure on the roads of America. We put our faith in a lot of strangers and a few friends and relatives along the way. We still have our diary from that escapade and it reflects the warm, good-natured spirit of the American people.

Would I recommend such a trip to someone today? Probably not and that's unfortunate. Hitchhiking is more risky now than it was in 1964. Still, I wouldn't take anything for that daring experience. I discovered risk-taking is necessary for success to have a chance. I learned if you're willing to risk—and accept the consequences of those risks—then go for it!

On my office wall hangs this plaque. It really puts risk-taking in candid perspective:

The Man Who Dares
Author Unknown

> The man who decides what he wants to achieve
> And works till his dreams all come true,
> The man who will alter his course when he must
> And bravely begin something new.
> The man who's determined to make his world better
> Who's willing to learn and to lead,
> The man who keeps trying and doing his best
> Is the man who knows how to succeed.

61

Mistakes

"Experience is the name everyone gives to their mistakes."

— Oscar Wilde

■　■　■

I once saw these words on an office wall plaque: "I never make mistakes. I once thought I did, but I was wrong." What a great reminder that only the proud and foolish think they never make mistakes.

For whatever reasons, most people find it difficult to accept responsibility for their mistakes. Even small children are quick to blame others for their boo-boos. Teenagers tend to see everyone else's errors but their own.

Yet, a big part of growing up and becoming wiser is the realization that mistakes do happen. As my speaker friend W. Mitchell likes to say, "It's not what happens to you, it's what you do about it." Are you mastered by your mistakes or are you the master of your mistakes?

I remember my high school typing class. Initially, I couldn't do anything right on that keyboard. My papers were full of mistakes. However, by year's end, I was typing 60 words per minute with few mistakes. Later, I used this skill as an *Atlanta Constitution* sports writer and Associated Press staff writer.

Today, I still use my typing skills to produce many letters and articles for my business and other organizations.

But suppose I'd let those early typing class mistakes discourage me? What if I hadn't been determined to learn from my mistakes? Now, I'm making mistakes on my computer as I strive to become proficient on this technological marvel.

Mistakes are merely the bridges that must be crossed in pursuit of experience and wisdom. That doesn't mean mistakes are planned or welcomed. It simply means mistakes must be put in the proper perspective—as stepping stones to learning and growing, not stumbling blocks to ignorance and immaturity.

Alas, the biggest mistake of all is to never try for fear of making mistakes. Perhaps the poet Vachel Lindsay said it best in *Litany of the Heroes*: "God make our blunders wise."

62

Change

"The pain of every change is forgotten when the benefits of that change are realized."

— *Tom Hopkins*
How To Master The Art Of Selling

■ ■ ■

Change is an enigma. It can be both good and bad depending upon a person's viewpoint. Certain values and principles have remained relatively changeless throughout the history of civilization. On the other hand, consider the enormous changes that have occurred in the 20th century alone.

Technologically, we've gone from lanterns to electricity, and from wells to indoor water faucets. We've gone from mail that took days to deliver to instant communication by telephone and facsimile machines. We've gone from horse-drawn carriages to automobiles and supersonic airplanes, and from adding machines to highly sophisticated computers. The changes are mind-boggling.

We've been blessed in America with a Constitution and Bill of Rights that have remained virtually unchanged even though the leaders of our democratic form of government have changed many times. By contrast, Germany has witnessed Hitler's Nazi government; the split into East and West Germany and the Berlin Wall; and the merger of these two nations all in one century.

Likewise, czarist Russia became the USSR in 1917 as the communists came into power. Seventy-four years later, the communist regime crumbled and was replaced by a democratic government and a desire for a free market economy.

American business has seen enormous change. The mom and pop stores are a dying breed as they've been replaced by the K-Marts, Wal-Marts, Office Depots, Home Depots, Drug Emporiums, Cub Foods, McDonald's and thousands of other volume operators. Corporate loyalty is going by the wayside with so many mergers, leveraged buyouts, layoffs and early retirement packages. This has spawned a new generation of entrepreneurs specializing in highly niched markets.

Of course, some things never change. For example, each of us has one set of biological parents. We each have one hometown. We can't change our height once we've grown up. We can't change the weather. We can't change the aging process, although some people try to slow it down with cosmetic surgery.

Yes, change can be painful. Yet at times it may be necessary. Each of us must choose to embrace change or resist change. Quite often, the headache of changing isn't nearly as great as the heartache of not changing.

Frankly, most of the changes in my life have been for the best once I adjusted to the newness. I've found worrying about change is often more damaging than the change itself. As a rule, I find change creates excitement in life and keeps me from getting stuck in a rut.

What follows is a list of the most significant changes (or turning points) in my life and the resulting impact. Perhaps you might want to list your major turning points and look for the positive impact these changes have had on your life:

YEAR (AGE)	TURNING POINT	IMPACT
1960 (15)	Moved to Atlanta, Georgia.	Became a serious student and a more well-rounded person in a big city environment.
1963 (18)	Joined the Marine Corps.	Matured after dropping out of college; got to see the world.
1970 (25)	Entered the sales profession/married.	Career blossomed after leaving journalism. Settled down by marrying but never had children.
1973 (28)	Divorced.	A traumatic adjustment, but 11 years of bachelorhood taught me a lot about what I *didn't* want out of life.
1982 (37)	Started my own business. Met Judy.	Entrepreneurship agreed with my independent, creative nature. Judy rejuvenated my dormant spiritual life.
1984 (39)	Married Judy and became a stepfather to two young girls.	Proved to be a major adjustment, but also the most rewarding and satisfying experience of my life.
1986 (41)	Joined the National Speakers Association/ Georgia Speakers Association and launched the speaking/training side of my business.	Kept me in business and eventually led to the writing of this book.

Change

NOTE—A special thank you to Juanell Teague, the president of Dallas-based People Plus, Inc., for challenging me to think about these turning points. She made me realize we have to keep a long-term perspective about our lives while we're dealing with the challenge of change, especially in the critical turning point moments we all experience.

63

Making a Difference

"History is replete with heroic people who realized that they could make a difference, and did—despite the conventional wisdom of the day."
— *Theodore Hesburgh*
God, Country, Notre Dame

■ ■ ■

Let's face it. In a free enterprise system like America, making money is important. However, making a difference is more important if we want to live life to its fullest.

Unfortunately, we often let the enormity of a task or the negative thinking of others deter us from striving to make a difference. The biggest tragedy is to assume we can't make any difference whatsoever. In truth, we can exert incredible influence on the lives of others, but the results of our efforts aren't always apparent until later.

For example, my parents served as Salvation Army officers from 1948-52 in Weirton, a community in the panhandle of West Virginia across from Steubenville, Ohio. The pay was minimal, the hours were long, the demands were considerable and the stress was immense. But Salvation Army officers are called to serve God through others, so that's what Captain and Mrs. Biggs did in this steel town along the banks of the Ohio River. When they were reassigned to a new appointment in Cumberland, Maryland,

it prompted a poignant column in the *Weirton Daily Times*
by Millie Martin. In part, it said:

"This morning my phone rang off the wall. 'What's
this I hear about Captain Biggs leaving?' was the
repeated question. Each caller demanded to know
why he was being taken out of Weirton, and wanted
to know if anything could be done to keep him here.
During my 10 years with the newspaper, a number
of ministers and prominent men have come and gone
in this community . . . but never before have so
many people been so concerned about a person
departing from Weirton.

And the answer is simple. Captain Daniel Biggs
has made a deep and lasting impression on the
people of this thriving town. Once in a while a
person moves into a town and through his noble
characteristics, understanding, sympathetic nature,
sincere spirit of service and deep interest in his
fellow men, enriches the lives of all those with
whom he comes in contact. And so it has been with
Captain Biggs, who not only has served The Salvation Army well . . . but has also served the people of
this community and country above and beyond the
call of duty.

It would be impossible to give full credit to the
work of this humble and modest man, who has made
Weirton a better place in which to live through his
unselfish service and ministry. Not only did Captain
Biggs greatly expand the growth of The Salvation
Army and secure for its members a long-envisioned
and urgently needed citadel, but he took an active
part in every worthwhile program in the community.
This soft-spoken man had a way of getting things
done for his church, his people and for all the
unfortunate people who came seeking help.

I know how this man of God extended help to others when they were denied help from other sources due to restrictions, red tape and lack of concern. It would be impossible for me to number the calls I personally made to the Captain when other sources of help failed. Not once did he say, 'I can't' or 'I'll try.' He always took care of the problem at once despite the difficulty. There were no alibis. Men of Captain Biggs' calibre . . . don't walk into a community every day."

In 1992, my sister Carol Johnson returned to Weirton to visit some of the Salvation Army people my parents served 40 years ago. "They were still talking about Captain and Mrs. Biggs," said Carol, "and how much they meant to Weirton." Joe Powell, a loyal Salvation Army member in Weirton, named his son Daniel, who then named his son Daniel in honor of my father. What a tribute to making a difference.

64

Encouragement Is Empowerment

"People have a way of becoming what you encourage them to be—not what you nag them to be."
                                        — *Scudder N. Parker*

■ ■ ■

I mentioned in Chapter 37 that I got my job as an Associated Press (AP) writer due to a strike by the writers and teletype operators. What I didn't tell you is I never joined the AP union. Naturally, I was branded as a "scab."

Every AP employee had a mail slot. On many occasions my slot would be filled with negative, anonymous notes about my failure to join the union. Fortunately, my slot would also be filled with positive notes from Lamar Matthews, my news editor.

Mr. Matthews was an encourager. He always took the time to review my previous day's work. He'd point out my shortcomings, which were many in the beginning, but he'd do so in a kind and caring way. More importantly, Mr. Matthews would tell me what I had done right. I still have those reviews and treasure them like gold. Here are some examples:

March 7, 1969

"Your copy is better than we normally get from a beginner, but you need a good bit of work. In general, you seem to be straining—trying too hard to write according to some preconceived formula. You'll overcome this if you work at it. Tell it simply, clearly and smoothly."

March 20, 1969

"Your copy is becoming much more readable and the style errors called to your attention earlier are being eliminated. You still occasionally use too many words, but generally you're showing good improvement. But I must emphasize the importance of accuracy. Check the facts; use care in rewriting; get it right."

April 8, 1969

"You are to be commended for steady improvement, both in writing and in elimination of style and other mistakes. Please continue to fire away with any questions or let me know if I can help in any way."

April 16, 1969

"Your output last night leaves little doubt about carrying your share of the load. In addition to writing a hefty chunk of the morning copy, I note you did 18 out of 25 evening stories. You've reached the point where speed and volume should be no drawback. Now polish to perfection."

Through his encouraging words, Lamar Matthews empowered me to do better each day despite the nasty notes I received from some of my fellow employees. At the tender age of 23, his encouragement helped me do a tough job in what was often a negative environment. Thank you

---

for your encouraging words, Mr. Matthews. It was a great
lesson in empowerment.

65

Teamwork

"The team player knows that the team comes first. It doesn't matter who gets the credit as long as the job gets done. If the job gets done, the credit will come."
— Howard E. Ferguson
The Edge

■　■　■

I don't believe it's a fluke that team-building is one of the most desired training topics within corporate America. While individual recognition is a part of team cohesiveness, it's important to realize that unless the company (team) succeeds, any individual triumphs will be bittersweet. When the company (team) succeeds, a good leader will find the time to reward the employees (players).

Perhaps the best examples of teamwork in society are demonstrated within the sporting world. In sports such as baseball, basketball or football, each player's special talents enable the team to work toward a common purpose of playing up to their God-given ability. As a result, greater goals are achieved as a team than any one individual could hope to accomplish—the winning of a championship, for example.

Even in individual sports such as boxing or gymnastics, no athlete can accomplish anything worthwhile without the help of others. For example, an Olympic gymnast performing solo on a balance beam only four inches in width could

not compete for a gold medal without the help of support-
ive parents and friends, knowledgeable and dedicated
coaches, first-rate competition and the financial support of
many corporations. The athlete's peak performance is a
product of teamwork.

The biggest enemy of the team concept is excessive
individual pride. One overinflated ego has destroyed the
morale and effectiveness of many talented ball clubs. On
the other hand, a less talented club can accomplish extra-
ordinary feats when individual recognition is surrendered
for the good of the team.

Ironically, the letters "me" are a part of the word team.
However, it takes more than the letters "me" to spell team.
In truth, no one can accomplish anything worthwhile
without the cooperation of others. We are only able to do
what we do because of the thousands of teams that have
paved the way for our success. Our individual achievements
are undeniably linked to the synergistic spirit of teams such
as our family, school, church, military, business community,
social organizations and many others.

Remember, teamwork is the skillful coordination of
individual efforts directed towards the collective efficiency
of the group. Without the interdependence of these teams,
life would be too difficult and individual successes would
be extremely limited.

66

Punctuality

"A person who is habitually late has no respect for another person's time."

— *Daniel K. Biggs*

■ ■ ■

When Rebecca and Tara, my stepdaughters, started going out with their teenage friends, I'd always tell them to be in my midnight. I didn't mean 12:02 or 12:10. I meant 12 o'clock sharp.

To ensure this deadline was met, I had a simple rule. Each minute of tardiness was equal to 15 minutes off the deadline for the next outing. In other words, come in at 12:15 a.m. and that meant coming in at 8:15 p.m. the next time. I rarely had a problem with the girls' punctuality.

Tara recently told me several things she learned growing up. At the top of the list was "the importance of being on time." I learned the same lesson as a youngster from my father Daniel K. Biggs. He deplored being late.

If cleanliness is next to Godliness, then surely timeliness is a good choice to complete a special triumvirate. People who are always late are rude. It's a bad habit that reflects a lack of foresight.

I realize there are times when tardiness is beyond our control. If an airplane doesn't take off on time or the traffic isn't moving, schedules can get sidetracked. However, most scheduling is within our control. It's a matter of being considerate of the time constraints of other people. Frankly, habitual tardiness is a selfish act.

What happens so often is we expect people to be late based on past experiences. As a result, a meeting never starts on time because "some of our people are always late." Once this precedent is set, it can be difficult to overcome.

I'm grateful my father taught me the importance of punctuality. I'm especially happy Rebecca and Tara think it's a valuable lesson as well. It's not that being late a time or two is so bad—it isn't. But when one tardiness leads to another and another, the danger is in lateness becoming a bad habit and marking a person as irresponsible and unreliable.

Here are a few tips for developing or improving the good habit of promptness:

- ▶ Regardless of the appointment, be determined to arrive on time. Otherwise, it's easy to fall into the trap of arriving promptly for the "important" engagements and arriving late for all the others.

- ▶ Think through the details of each day's schedule the previous evening. Planning now can save a lot of time and embarrassment later.

- ▶ Always anticipate unexpected delays. If it takes 30 minutes to get somewhere, allow 45 minutes or an hour depending upon the time of day. Any spare minutes can always be used wisely, but it's impossible to reclaim lost time.

67

Politeness

"Politeness is the hallmark of the gentleman and the gentle-woman. No characteristic will so help one to advance, whether in business or society, as politeness."
— *B. C. Forbes*

If a little courtesy goes a long way, then consider these suggestions as you go about your daily activities:

- If you're a smoker, be considerate of others in public places. Smoking annoys non-smokers and it's harmful to everyone.

- Control your tongue in public places. Most likely, someone will be offended by profanity and it doesn't speak well for the person using such language.

- Screen the jokes and stories you tell in public. Dirty ones may get a laugh, but so will clean humor.

- Drink alcohol in public only if you can control your behavior. And don't drink and drive period!

- Remember courtesy when driving. Pretend all the other drivers are your next door neighbors. (And do wear your seat belts and get rid of those speed detection devices!)

- Take the time to hold open a door for someone, help somebody up a flight of stairs or lighten a load for a stranger. It's time well spent. Besides, you'll appreciate the same courtesy when it's extended to you.

- ► When you ask a question, let the person answer without interruption.

- ► Schedule meetings only when they are purposeful. Start on time, follow an agenda, get to the point, make decisions and end on time.

- ► In conversation, take turns. Instead of dominating a conversation by boasting of your accomplishments, try asking other people what they think or how they feel, then listen politely.

- ► Keep confidential or potentially damaging information to yourself. Remember, gossip ends up hurting everyone involved.

- ► Do return telephone calls. No one should be *that* busy!

- ► Do try to smile and speak to everyone you meet. It's truly amazing how far a little hospitality will go.

68

Tact

"Tact: The ability to tell a man he's open-minded when he has a hole in his head."

— *F. G. Kernan*

■ ■ ■

Diplomats are known for their ability to say and do things in an inoffensive manner. However, it's a skill anyone would do well to master. Tactful people are poised people. Interestingly, a synonym for poise is the word balance.

I was privileged to serve as a Marine security guard at the American embassies in Warsaw and Rome in the 1960s. A part of our training for this prestigious duty included courses in protocol and diplomacy. In effect, we were front-line ambassadors for our country since a part of our responsibility was access control for anyone entering or departing the embassy.

Since embassies deal with some very sensitive international issues, it's vital that all personnel think through a situation and consider the feelings of all parties involved before speaking or acting. Tact is a trait as instinctive to a diplomat as reflexes are to an athlete.

While other careers might not be quite as sensitive as the diplomatic field, I believe tact is necessary for long-term success in any endeavor. Why? Because people simply won't tolerate abrasive, arrogant behavior without feeling a sense of animosity and hostility.

A little tact is like a dose of smelling salts—it goes a long way and is usually very effective. People like to be treated with respect and dignity. A quick slip of the tongue can strain the strongest relationships and undermine the common purpose of any organization.

In reality, tact is nothing more than the Golden Rule in action. It's merely exercising a little common sense in your relationships with others. It's understanding why discretion is a more valued personality trait than disrespect. It's realizing words are weapons and should be used carefully.

The insight of Publilius Syrus, circa 42 B.C., is as relevant today as it was more than 2,000 years ago when he addressed the subject of tact: "Let a fool hold his tongue and he will pass for a sage." (Maxim 914)

69

Goodwill

"Goodwill: The disposition of a customer to return to the place where he/she has been well treated."
— *U.S. Supreme Court*
(Interpretation of goodwill)

■ ■ ■

No matter what position you hold in your company, you're a goodwill ambassador for that organization. Everything you think, say and especially do ultimately determines how many of your customers return because they've been well treated.

I've often heard employees say sales or marketing or public relations or customer service isn't their job. That kind of closed-minded attitude will surely hasten the day of a company's closing. In today's competitive business world, you simply can't survive without building goodwill at all levels within a company.

On the other hand, take a look at the businesses that are thriving. All employees are trained continuously in the art of satisfying the customer. It's such a simple concept. A paycheck does not come from one's company, it comes from the company's customers!

Building goodwill is an ongoing process observed daily by every employee working as a team. Any successful team striving to build goodwill must have a (1) common purpose,

(2) meaningful interaction and communication and (3) shared results.

The common purpose should be to serve your customers in the best manner possible. The meaningful interaction and communication occurs in the hundreds of daily activities that transpire between the employees and the customers seeking the products and services of a company. The shared results are manifested in individual compensation and company profits, and the recognition of a job well done.

As a business owner, I've always maintained an attitude that it's better to solve a problem than to avoid one. Customers are looking for professional problem-solvers, so I view problems as opportunities to build goodwill. I've discovered it's more economical to keep an old customer than to find a new one. Generally, if I take care of my customers, they'll take care of me.

John Wesley, the founder of Methodism, knew all about goodwill and customer service. His 18th century advice should be the motto of every business:

John Wesley's Rule

> Do all the good you can,
> By all the means you can,
> In all the ways you can,
> In all the places you can,
> At all the times you can,
> To all the people you can,
> As long as ever you can.

70

Dependability

"The greatest ability is dependability."

— Anonymous

■ ■ ■

The only thing more frustrating than dealing with an unreliable person is dealing with someone who justifies their unreliability by saying, "I'm not perfect, you know!" Perfection is not the issue since everyone makes mistakes. The issue is dependability, which is something an imperfect human being can develop into a good habit.

Dependability is a statement of a person's character in action. A person's word isn't good enough if actions don't follow. Integrity isn't possible without dependability. A Code of Ethics is only as good as the person who applies these worthwhile principles in daily living.

What does it take to be dependable? It requires congruency between words and action. It means "walking the talk." It means being able to be counted on in every situation within human control.

Obviously, there are always going to be exceptions. For example, plans can go awry due to a death in the family, illness, a delayed airline flight, inclement weather, a traffic accident or a natural disaster. People understand these situations provided they're given an honest explanation.

The problem lies in habitually making poor excuses for unreliability. Alas, excuses become reasons not to do something as promised. It's disrespectful of another person and their time. It's also a poor reflection on the character of the person trying to justify their unreliability.

Quite often dependability is a matter of not taking on too many tasks. A part of balance is knowing when to say no to one task so more pressing projects can be fulfilled as agreed. Essentially, it's better to do a few things well than to be stretched too thinly and perform in an unreliable manner.

Dependability is a skill anyone can learn with enough practice. Respect is earned, for the most part, by the degree of a person's dependability. As Andy Hillman, a former sales manager of mine, likes to say of reliable people: "You can set your watch by them."

Practice and
Attention to Detail

"What I hear, I forget. What I see, I remember. But what I do, I understand."

— *Confucius*
(451 B.C.)

■ ■ ■

I'll never forget my first morning at Marine Corps boot camp at Parris Island, South Carolina—October 16, 1964. It was pitch dark and our ragtag Platoon, No. 295, was standing in line waiting for orders to enter the 2nd Battalion mess hall. We were still in our civilian clothes.

To the rear of our platoon, I heard the unforgettable, rhythmic sound of thud . . . thud . . . thud . . . thud . . . thud! I turned to see what was making this awesome sound. I discovered a veteran platoon marching in perfect cadence. The thud sound was the striking of 75 boot heels against the asphalt street.

Unfortunately, the drill instructor of the veteran platoon saw me admiring his troops. He raced to my side, put his mouth down over my ear and uttered these memorable words: "Why are you looking at MY platoon, boy? Are you queer for MY platoon or what?"

Actually, I was in awe of his platoon marching in such splendid precision. Would our platoon be able to do that?

I soon learned such precision was the result of endless hours of practice on the parade deck. The attention to detail was so meticulous a drill instructor's sharp eyes could spot one recruit marching out of step in a platoon of 75.

By the end of our 12 weeks of recruit training, Platoon 295 was marching like the veteran platoon I'd witnessed my first morning at Parris Island. We were a well-oiled team because of attention to detail and lots of practice.

Generally, most activities don't consist of one major task, but rather a series of small details that shape the end results. For example, one of the highlights of Marine boot camp is the drill competition in the final week of training. The numerous close order drills, the manual of arms and the instant obedience to commands are practiced for weeks until each exercise becomes second nature. Of course, the end product is a drill competition performed by a Marine platoon executing a series of synchronized drills in perfect harmony.

To get things done more efficiently and effectively, pay attention to the details, master each one with rigorous practice and you'll be a true professional.

72

Results

"The result proves the wisdom of the act."

— *Ovid*
(43 B.C. - A.D. 18)

■ ■ ■

We hear a lot these days about the bottom line. Quite often, results are measured only in dollars and cents. Have we forgotten about top line results?

Top line results are measured in terms of people. An organization's top line is its employees and customers, which generates a bottom line profit. Without a strong top line, there is no profitable bottom line!

While this basic premise is well understood—that only people can generate monetary results—why is it so many organizations place more value on profitability than people? Doesn't it make sense that well-trained, highly motivated and properly compensated employees will produce a ripple effect that carries from the top of an organization down to bottom line profitability?

For example, look at what's happened to the automobile industry in the 1980s and early 1990s. Manufacturers have produced too many automobiles and established too many dealerships. Profits have been squeezed as the cost of automobiles have soared far beyond the average household income.

In their zeal to sell more cars and restore profitability, many manufacturers haven't selected the best dealership owners. In turn, some dealerships have produced misleading advertising campaigns. They've attracted poor quality sales and management teams. The results: high turnover, low ethics, poor or non-existent training, a poor image and disgruntled customers. When you couple all of this with hard-sell, high pressure sales tactics, is it any wonder why bottom line results have suffered?

In the long haul, you win with good people and you make money with good people—in that order! The automobile industry is starting to accept this reality as most manufacturers are offering quality training to their dealerships. The National Automobile Dealers Association (NADA) has launched a sales certification program to upgrade the ethics and education of dealership sales and management teams. Many dealerships are eliminating deceptive sales and financing tactics and treating their customers with respect and dignity.

Because the automobile industry not only understands its problems but is now acting upon them, their bottom line results should improve dramatically due to a significant refinement of its top line. The lesson is crystal clear. Invest wisely in quality people for top line results, then watch your bottom line prosper.

73

Commitment

"A life without surrender is a life without commitment."
— *Jerry Rubin*
Growing (Up) At 37

■ ■ ■

What we say is mighty important, but what we do is what counts!

How many times has a person said "consider it done" only to have the words ring hollow when the job doesn't get done? Undoubtedly, there are many reasons why promises aren't converted into productivity. Yet, each time we make a promise and fail to keep it, we chip away at our credibility.

Perhaps the biggest difference between what we say and what we do is the word commitment. It's a frequently used word, but do we really understand the real meaning? Webster's defines commitment as "an agreement or pledge to do something in the future . . . the state of being obligated."

Reliability and trust are the essence of commitment. Thus, what we say won't be the loudest voice in the commitment equation—what we do will! We become reliable and trustworthy people based on the way we fulfill our promises. Anyone can make a promise, but only a committed person will deliver on their promises.

In Ecclesiastes 5:5 (GNV), we're told: "Better not to promise at all than to make a promise and not keep it." Needless to say, we should exercise extreme caution in the verbal obligations we undertake. It's much better to underpromise and overdeliver than to overpromise and underdeliver. Perhaps the best time management tool of all is the ability to say no so we don't overcommit.

On my office wall hangs a plaque bearing these words by an anonymous author:

Commitment

Commitment is what transforms a promise into a reality. It is the words that speak boldly of your intentions. And the actions which speak louder than words.

It is making the time when there is none. Coming through time after time, year after year after year.

Commitment is the stuff character is made of; the power to change the face of things.

It is the daily triumph of integrity over skepticism.

What is at stake? Your "daily triumph of integrity over skepticism."

74

Perseverance

*"Genius, that power which dazzles mortal eyes, is oft
but perseverance in disguise."*

— *Henry Willard Austin*
Perseverance Conquers All

■ ■ ■

In the course of human history, I wonder how many
millions of people have failed to accomplish a goal when
the end was just around the next corner? By contrast, I'm
curious how many millions of people have achieved a goal
primarily on sheer stubbornness? Indeed, there's a fine line
between success and failure. Perseverance is often the
biggest difference.

Since forming my company in 1982, I've come close to
quitting on several occasions. However, the spring of 1989
was my biggest crisis. My automobile leasing business was
declining. My lease training business was still in its growth
stage after less than two years.

In addition to declining income, I was spending a lot of
money promoting the training side of my business. I had
a serious cash flow problem. How serious? My $50,000
business line of credit was at its limit. I'd delved into a
large portion of our personal savings. The entrepreneurial
picture was looking mighty dim.

On May 24, 1989, I was scheduled to do one of my
local lease training seminars. Since late 1987, I'd been

mailing out promotional brochures to all the Atlanta automobile dealerships, then calling to secure enough people for two classes per month. The typical attendance was about 20 people at $95 per head. A recent attendee had been George Spears, general manager of Capital Cadillac.

George told Joe Fetzer about my May 24 session. Joe was the Cadillac Southeast Zone Manager. He invited Jim Clark, who was Cadillac's East Coast Marketing Manager at the time. The day before they were to attend this seminar, I lost about 10 attendees when one dealership canceled. Six others no-showed on the morning of the seminar. I was left with two Cadillac executives (no charge) and one Ford dealership salesman ($95, which didn't even cover the meeting room cost).

Have you ever conducted a seminar for three people? As a speaker who thrives on the energy of an audience, it's awfully tough to lead a seminar with so few people. In addition, I was concerned the Cadillac executives would frown on hiring someone who couldn't draw any bigger crowd than three people. On the other hand, if I could land the national lease training account of Cadillac, it could turn my business around.

I decided to do the best job I could that day in spite of the poor attendance and the financial loss. It must have worked because Joe Fetzer and Jim Clark took me to lunch after the seminar. I began a series of national seminars for Cadillac in August, 1989 that lasted a year. This account led to the Infiniti account, which led to the Nissan account, which led to the Honda account and many others.

What made me persevere in spite of tremendous financial pressure? I'm sure the fear of having to go back to work for someone else was certainly a big motivator. More than anything, though, I persevered because I believed in what I was doing. I knew I had a needed service. I felt it was only a matter of time before my investment would start to pay dividends.

75

Experience

"Experience is knowing a lot of things you shouldn't do."

— *William S. Knudsen*

■ ■ ■

Experience is a perplexity. A person can't gain experience without an opportunity, but often the opportunity isn't provided due to a person's inexperience. So just how is experience acquired?

Experience is a series of building blocks. For example, I learned my ABCs as a small child. I began to put simple sentences together in elementary school. I developed my writing skills in high school. By my senior year, I was editor of the school newspaper.

I went to work as a copy boy at *The Atlanta Constitution* a few months before my high school graduation. This opportunity led to a job as a sports writing intern. I continued to hone my writing skills in the Marine Corps. After my discharge, I took a job as a staff writer for the Associated Press.

When I decided to leave journalism for sales in 1970, I used my writing experience as a marketing tool to gain new customers and secure repeat business and referrals. In 1982, I started my own business and soon launched a company newsletter. Since then, I've had numerous articles published in trade journals, which have helped establish me as an expert in my field. As a result, training became an integral part of my business.

The book you hold in your hands is no accident. It's the product of endless writing experiences since I was a kid. I started with small writing projects and built on those experiences—one by one. Sure, I've made a lot of mistakes along the way, but I've persisted because I love to write. It's my passion.

Find out what you love to do and gain as much experience as possible. No experience is too small if you're seeking excellence in what you do. Each experience opens another window of opportunity as you build on your successes and learn from your failures.

There is absolutely no substitute for experience and it can only be attained in due time. We're a product of all the activities we choose to participate in over a lifetime. However, the experience of a 60-year-old simply can't be acquired in 20 years.

In this "To Do" section, I've tried to share some of the more valuable qualities that, if honed, can help anyone achieve more while maintaining a reasonable measure of balance in their life. That's why I admire Abigail Van Buren's philosophy on experience: "If we could sell our experiences for what they cost, we'd all be millionaires."

PART IV

"TO HAVE"

The Emotional Force

"Happiness is not getting what you want, but wanting what you have."

— *Anonymous*

76

A God of Grace

". . . for all have sinned and fall short of the glory of God, and are justified freely by His grace through the redemption that came by Christ Jesus."
— *Romans 3:23-24 (NIV)*

■ ■ ■

Despite all the human suffering in the world, I have a God of grace. How can that possibly be true? Why doesn't a God of grace put an end to war, crime, poverty, hunger, disease and many other social injustices?

First, mankind caused its own downfall by rebelling against the Creator in the Garden of Eden. Only a God of grace would give us the free will to choose between good and evil. Adam and Eve chose evil and this disobedience led to the suffering of mankind (Genesis 3:16-19).

Next, only a God of grace would have instructed Noah to place two of every living creature on an ark in order to survive the Great Flood. Only a God of grace would have given the Ten Commandments to Moses. Only a God of grace would have sent the Old Testament prophets to predict humankind's deliverance.

Finally, only a God of grace would have sent his only son Jesus Christ to die on the cross that mankind might be saved and have eternal life. God has been in control since the Creation, but humanity has turned its back on God's laws and especially God's grace. Only a God of grace would provide a plan for our salvation with the advance knowledge we would stray from that divine plan.

The good news is no matter what our sins are—and we've all sinned—a God of grace still loves us enough to forgive us of our sins. How do we receive such forgiveness? We simply must *confess* our sins (Psalms 32:5), *repent* of our sins (Acts 2:38) and *believe* in Jesus Christ (Acts 13:28).

The only thing God's grace will not accept is the unrepentant sinner. Yet, throughout civilization, men and women have rebelled against God. Because we have the freedom to choose between good and evil, God does not impose his will upon us. Thus, the destiny of your own soul is determined by a simple choice—God's way and eternal life or the way of sin and eternal suffering.

God is with us in our earthly struggles. God sent His Son to suffer on the cross that we might be released from suffering. By accepting Jesus Christ as your personal Savior, you'll be freed from the worst suffering of all— eternal separation from God!

77

Eternal Life

"For God so loved the world that he gave his one and only Son, that whoever believes in him shall not perish but have eternal life."

— John 3:16 (NIV)

■ ■ ■

If you're a Christian, the above verse is one of the best known in the New Testament. If you're not a Christian, most everyone has pondered the question, "What happens to me when I die?"

I happen to be a Methodist. However, I don't believe in coercing anyone into accepting my particular religious faith. By the same token, I firmly believe the words Jesus Christ spoke to Nicodemus, a member of the Jewish ruling council, in John 3:16. I hope you believe this passage as well and here's why.

Suppose you choose not to believe in Jesus Christ as the Son of God and this passage proves to be true. What then? On the other hand, suppose you do believe in Jesus Christ as the Son of God and this passage proves to be untrue. What have you lost by trying to live a God-fearing, Christ-centered life while on earth?

You see, I don't believe something as miraculous as a human being simply evolved. I believe God created us in His own image despite the fact we've failed to live up to the high standards God envisioned for us. Moreover, I

---

believe God will reward those who heed the words of John 3:16. What could be more rewarding than eternal life?

Growing up in The Salvation Army, I heard many sermons pose this forthright question, "Where will you spend eternity?" Some refer to this as "fire and brimstone" preaching. As I've grown older, I've found it impossible to ignore such a soul-searching question. I must answer such a probing question.

I intend to spend eternity in heaven. That doesn't mean I have to live a perfect life while on earth. It simply means I have to believe the words of John 3:16. As Dr. L. Nelson Bell, the father-in-law of evangelist Billy Graham, once said: "Only those who are prepared to die are really prepared to live."

While I want to live a long, healthy and meaningful life on this earth, I'm prepared to die. I know in dying I'll live forever. Prior to raising Lazarus from the dead, Jesus said to Martha, the sister of Lazarus: "I am the resurrection and the life. He who believes in me will live, even though he dies; and whoever lives and believes in me will never die. Do you believe this?" (John 11:25-26, NIV)

Do you?

78

A Church Home

"Bless all the churches, and blessed be God, who, in this our great trial, giveth us the churches."
— Abraham Lincoln
To a Methodist delegation
May 14, 1864

■ ■ ■

Since my parents were Salvation Army officers, I not only was raised in the church, but we actually lived next to or above the church until I was 12 years old. For me, the church wasn't just a Sunday service—it was a way of life.

In 1964, I joined the Marine Corps and my church activities came to an abrupt halt. I figured I'd get active again after my discharge four years later. It didn't happen. In fact, I experienced a 19-year void in my church life.

Oh, I would go to church for a wedding, a funeral or an occasional Christmas or Easter service. Otherwise, I would find every excuse not to attend. I was out late Saturday night. I didn't want to get up early Sunday morning and put on a suit. I was out of town. I had something else to do.

I knew I should be attending church. At times, I felt a deep sense of guilt. Finally, on December 15, 1982, I met Judy, who would become my wife nearly two years later. Judy let me know how important church was to her. Gradually, I began to attend services. Now, I wonder why I stayed away so long.

Having a church home doesn't make me any better than someone who doesn't belong to a church. Like any other group of people, a church is comprised of imperfect human beings struggling with the same difficulties of life as people who aren't church members. So why bother to go to church? Aren't they all just a bunch of hypocrites anyway?

Every organization has its share of dissemblers. Jim Bakker and Jimmy Swaggart gave religion a black eye. Leona Helmsley (hotels), Ivan Boesky (investments), Charles Keating (savings & loan) and Gary Hart (politics) were a disappointment to their peers and to the American people. While these high-profile stories make the headlines, there are millions of honest, hard working people seeking to serve their respective organizations in anonymity and with integrity.

I go to church because it's the Lord's house. I go to church because I enjoy the Christian camaraderie. I go to church for spiritual refuge and serenity. I go to church to give of my time, talents and treasures for the betterment of others. I go to church to pray, sing, read the Bible and listen to my pastor's message of hope and inspiration.

I'm grateful to my parents for the spiritual training they provided as a child. Moreover, I'm indebted to Judy for the spiritual rejuvenation she helped spark within me as an adult. It's never too late to have a church home.

79

A Sense of Stewardship

When John Templeton, the acknowledged dean of global investing, was asked to name the best investment he'd ever made, he replied, ". . . the most risk-free investment, the most rewarding investment, was tithing. It means giving 10 percent of your income to the church and charities. I have never known anyone who regretted that investment."

■ ■ ■

Tithing is Biblical. Yet, the temptation is often to keep as much for ourselves and give away as little as possible. In reality, everything we have belongs to God. We're merely stewards of the bountiful riches we've been given.

The word steward means manager or caretaker. Stewardship is simply the wise management of what we have. In other words, a good steward is more concerned with the prudent *use* of money than its mere accumulation.

I first read John Templeton's advice about tithing in a column written by Nick Poulos of *The Atlanta Constitution* on October 23, 1986. I was particularly impressed with this statement by Templeton: "I have never known anyone who has made that investment for 10 years without being rewarded with both happiness and prosperity."

Soon after, I heard a stirring sermon on tithing by Dr. Malone Dodson, senior minister at our church—Roswell United Methodist in Roswell, Georgia. Dr. Dodson posed an interesting question: "Why is it we think nothing of tipping 15-20 percent to a waiter or waitress we'll probably never see again, but we question giving at least 10 percent to the church and worthwhile charities?"

The following week I was riding with Earl Masters, a friend, who was talking about his church's tremendous growth. Earl said this was possible due to an unusually high percentage of tithers within his church. When I asked Earl what he really thought about the concept of tithing, he uttered these memorable words: "If you'll give at least 10 percent of your income to the Lord's work, he'll pour on so many blessings you'll be amazed. You can't outgive God."

John Templeton, Malone Dodson and Earl Masters convinced Judy and me to tithe. We began on January 1, 1987. We give better than 10 percent of our gross annual income to our church and a few charities. I don't say this to boast, but to substantiate Mr. Templeton's advice that tithing is the best investment we've ever made.

In addition to the joy and fulfillment of helping others, we've actually witnessed a dramatic improvement in our personal financial picture. Now, please understand we don't give to get. Nevertheless, Luke 6:38 (GNV) says: "Give to others, and God will give to you." We just decided to give generously and trusted God to take care of everything else.

Stewardship is an outward sign of an inward commitment. Nonetheless, it's a difficult commitment for many people to embrace as reflected in a Gallup poll of 2,775 Americans. Households with incomes below $10,000 contribute to charity an average of 2.8 percent of their incomes. By contrast, households with incomes between $50,000 and $100,000 give an average of only 1.5 percent; and households with incomes of more than $100,000 donate an average of 2.1 percent of their incomes.

Could your sense of stewardship use an overhaul? Remember, "you can't outgive God." Amen!

80

Spiritual Influence

"Our attitude toward our fellow men is a more accurate gauge of our religion than all of our religious rantings."

— *Billy Graham*
The Secret Of Happiness

■ ■ ■

Of all the things I could have in this world, I'd want to know my life helped influence others in their spiritual relationship with God. No other gift has more lasting value or more impact on a person's quality of life.

Undeniably, it's one thing to talk about religion to others and quite another to live a religious life. Our actions tend to influence people a lot more than our words. Thus, the challenge is to internalize what we believe so that our actions deliver a more influential message than our expressions.

The one common thread of all religions is the Golden Rule. If we treat others the way we'd like to be treated, we set a marvelous example of religion in action. On the other hand, if we profess religion and act selfishly and irresponsibly, we make a mockery of the very religion we espouse.

One of the best ways to demonstrate spiritual influence is not by preaching, but rather in humbly serving your community. When is the last time you worked in a soup kitchen to feed the homeless? When is the last time you visited the elderly at a retirement or nursing home? When is the last time you took some underprivileged kids to a ball game or amusement park? When is the last time you volunteered to raise money for a charitable cause?

What better gift can a person give to another in a lifetime than a spiritual foundation? When death beckons, will anyone be wishing for another day at the office, greater material wealth or more prestige? Those things won't matter, but the spiritual roots we've helped nurture in others will be viable long after we're gone.

I'm reminded of the words of Hodding Carter, Jr., a Pulitzer Prize-winning Mississippi editor, who said: "There are two lasting bequests we can give our children. One is roots. The other is wings." My parents took painstaking care to plant my spiritual roots and I'm deeply grateful. When it was time to spread my wings and leave the nest, they understood.

Unfortunately, I used my newly acquired freedom to soar into some dangerous areas. I made some mistakes. I failed to use good judgment on several occasions. Eventually, it was my spiritual root system, along with the gentle influence of my wife, that enabled me to refocus on what's really important in life. I love Dad, Mom and Judy for that.

Whose lives are you spiritually influencing? Remember, the length of your life isn't nearly as important as the depth and breadth of your life.

81

A Free, Just Nation

". . . one Nation under God, indivisible, with liberty and justice for all."
— *Pledge of Allegiance to the flag of the United States of America*

■ ■ ■

In America, we enjoy abundant blessings because we have a free society and free enterprise. Our Constitution guarantees us freedoms such as religion, press, assembly and speech. While our system isn't perfect, it has worked exceedingly well since 1776.

There's a lot of talk about the declining America. Yes, we have problems with our economy, the erosion of moral values, racial prejudice, crime and many other concerns. Yet, people from all over the world still rush to our shores because freedom provides opportunity. I'd venture to say that most of these new Americans don't believe we're in a decline!

At the heart of the Soviet Union breakup was a struggle for the freedoms we take for granted in America. The former Soviet Union and Eastern Europe are adapting to the ideas of the Western nations, led my America. That's a sure sign a free society and free enterprise have defeated government suppression and communism.

Humankind was meant to be free. But freedom must be accompanied by justice or it's not complete freedom. The

Emancipation Proclamation gave freedom to the slaves in 1863. A century later, American blacks were still experiencing widespread social injustice.

Martin Luther King, Jr. led his non-violent crusade in the 1950s and 1960s to protest the plight of his people. While things have improved since King was killed in 1968, our justice system still has a long way to go in overcoming bigotry and social injustice.

Freedom gives people opportunity, but each individual is responsible for turning an opportunity into a worthwhile outcome. Justice ensures that opportunity isn't abused. Life isn't always fair, but a strong, effective judicial system is essential to prevent anarchy. Freedom only works when the people trust their government to enforce the laws in an equitable, honest and consistent manner.

Our forefathers came to America seeking freedom and justice from an oppressive English government. Since the Declaration of Independence was signed in 1776, America has prospered more than any nation in history. Many Americans have died to protect our precious freedoms, to see justice prevail. May we never forget the sacrifices that have been made in the name of "liberty and justice for all."

82

A Safe, Peaceful Community

"And for these ends to practice tolerance and live together in peace with one another as good neighbors."
— *From the Charter of the United Nations*

■ ■ ■

I've always admired the devotion of our law enforcement officers. They put their lives on the line every day to make our communities safe and peaceful. They do their jobs with little fanfare. They often work long and difficult hours. They earn far less than they're worth.

Despite the valiant efforts of our law enforcement agencies, many American communities are unsafe and in turmoil. The reasons are numerous—poverty, unemployment, drug abuse, gangs, violence, crime and on it goes. The human casualties are staggering. I don't believe this is the America envisioned by our forefathers.

Even if you live in a relatively safe, peaceful community, you're still at risk. Criminals bring their sinister ways to other neighborhoods to steal, vandalize, rape, harm and kill. As a result, we've witnessed the growth of neighborhood crime watches, elaborate security systems and scores of other products and services designed to make our communities safer and more peaceful.

I believe every American is entitled to a safe, serene community. If we're afraid to walk down our streets at night or if we dread leaving our homes unattended, something is dreadfully wrong with our society. Have we lost our sense of personal security?

I believe it's time to restore the dignity of the American community. This will require more than a vigilant police force. Peace officers can't be everywhere. It will require more than tough laws. Laws are often broken. It will require individual responsibility.

It's imperative that each individual respect the rights of everyone else in the community. It's critical for each individual to report any crimes or misconduct to the proper authorities. Moreover, it's vital that each individual realize a safe, peaceful community is a team effort.

America is nothing more than a reflection of the millions of communities which comprise this great nation. Each community is unique based upon its location, ethnic background, customs, mores, educational roots and economic situation. Despite these differences, each community deserves a safe, peaceful society in which to exercise such diverse lifestyles.

Are you doing all you can to ensure your community is safe and peaceful?

83

A Caring Family

"When families fail, society fails."
— *Former Vice President Dan Quayle*

■ ■ ■

The basic unit of society is the family. However, the American family has witnessed radical changes since the traditional family of the "Ozzie And Harriett" television series in the 1950s.

In those days, father was the undisputed leader of the family. He was usually the sole wage earner. As a rule, he remained with the same employer until retirement. Marriage was a lifetime commitment. Divorce was considered a social stigma, a last resort action. If the children disobeyed, father was the final authority for disciplinary action.

Mothers generally worked in the home. They performed all the household chores and cooked the meals. Moms were there for the children during the day and dispensed tender loving care in large doses. In the evenings, everyone participated in a variety of family activities. In short, a spirit of fellowship existed within the family and a strong values system emerged out of this process.

As we look at the evolvement of the typical American family into the 1990s, we see a strikingly different picture. It's not uncommon for both parents to be in the work force in order to make ends meet. One lifetime employer is a rarity and quite often at least one parent travels. Divorce is prevalent and single-parent families are widespread. Many children are using alcohol, cigarettes and drugs. Many teenagers have a casual attitude about sex, and youth gangs are spreading at an alarming rate.

I certainly didn't have a perfect family because my parents divorced about the time I was graduating from high school. Despite the marital struggles of my parents, I was loved, disciplined and taught traditional family values. I was encouraged to do well in school. I was involved in a variety of church activities. I didn't have the time nor the inclination to get into any major trouble.

Now that I'm a husband and stepfather, I'm grateful for the caring family I grew up in. I've tried to pass on some of the good things I learned from my parents and to learn from their mistakes. I can't change the reality of their divorce or that there's never been the same feeling of family closeness since that traumatic event occurred.

Nevertheless, I've tried to live my life in such a way that my parents can be proud of the results of their efforts. I've tried to set a worthy example for my wife and step-daughters. I believe I've succeeded thus far on both counts. How do I know?

I want to share a couple of Father's Day cards I've received since Rebecca and Tara have grown up and moved out on their own. From Rebecca Stvan: "I really love you a lot and can now truly appreciate all the times you would not let me go out. You only did it for my own good and now I realize that." From Tara Stvan: "You have been like a dad to me and I have learned many things from you. I am so glad my mom could find someone who cares about her as much as you do."

What do I have? I have a lot more than those cards. I have the incredible feeling of helping to mold the lives of two precious stepdaughters. I also have the marvelous memory of two parents who, despite their personal conflicts, helped shape my values and beliefs by providing special love, care and discipline.

84

A Special Spouse

"Choose your life's mate carefully. From this one decision will come 90 percent of all your happiness or misery."

— *H. Jackson Brown, Jr.*
Life's Little Instruction Book

■ ■ ■

I've always been fascinated with the reasons some marriages last and others don't.

My first marriage began on November 7, 1970. I was 25 years old and she was 22. On the marquee of the motel where I had breakfast with my father that morning was this prophetic message: "Love is blind, but marriage is the eye-opener!" Our marriage didn't make it quite three years.

In retrospect, we probably shouldn't have married. We had so many major differences to overcome. For most of the 11 years between my divorce and my marriage to Judy on August 4, 1984, I wondered if I'd ever meet that special woman. I knew what I wanted—and especially what I didn't want. I was determined to remain single rather than compromise on my choice of a lifetime mate.

Why is my second marriage so special? Primarily, we have so many *common interests* and we spend time sharing these interests. I'm not one to go out a lot with the guys because I'd rather be with Judy. Sure, there are times when we go our separate ways and I enjoy those moments. But overall, we love to do things together.

A major part of our common interests is our spiritual time. We pray together. We read and study the Bible together. We teach Sunday school together. We attend church together. We try our best to make God the focal point of our lives and to set a worthy example to others.

Besides common interests, we *communicate* regularly and openly. It's wonderful to have someone special to share in your successes and to listen when you've suffered setbacks. We feel like we can tell each other anything and we usually do. If you can't talk with your spouse, who can you talk to?

Finally, we *care* deeply about each other. We're always leaving each other little love notes and giving each other small tokens of appreciation. We don't assume our love will continue to grow. We make a daily effort to nurture love with simple, intimate expressions of our commitment to each other. We also care enough to be faithful to each other—a relationship built upon mutual trust and respect.

I'm so grateful I found Judy. She's smart, personable, attractive, sensitive, sweet, talented and caring—the absolute best wife a man could hope to have. I love you, sweetheart!

85

A Few Good Friends

"One friend in a life is much, two are many, three are hardly possible."

— *Henry Brooks Adams*
The Education Of Henry Adams

■ ■ ■

There's a big difference between acquaintances and friends. I have hundreds of acquaintances, but only a few good friends. So what are the qualities of a good friend?

Richard Barnfield (1574-1627) once said "faithful friends are hard to find . . . he that is thy friend, he will help thee in thy need." Good friends share in your successes and setbacks, but they especially rise to the occasion in a time of real need. They act unconditionally because they care, not because they expect the favor to be returned.

A good friendship usually requires time. That's not to say two people can't become good friends at once. However, most good friendships evolve as a result of many shared experiences. One experience builds upon another experience over a period of years.

Trust is as essential to a good friendship as a deep foundation is to a skyscraper. Things can be said in complete confidence since a good friend doesn't betray your trust. Trust and friendship are inseparable. Trust is the cement that holds the friendship together.

Good friends understand communications is a two-way street. They know when to talk and when to listen. They know when to give advice and when to seek advice. The lines of communications are always open and receptive to praise and constructive criticism.

Forgiveness is a must for any good friendship to thrive. Even the best of friends sometimes say and do things they didn't mean, especially in emotional and stressful situations. A good friend shows mercy because the friendship is more valuable than a singular moment in time.

Good friends must respect each other. I have the utmost respect for my wife. Consequently, that's a major reason why Judy is my best friend. Once mutual respect leaves a friendship, the relationship is doomed.

I don't think anyone said it more eloquently than Ralph Waldo Emerson in *Friendship*: "A friend may well be reckoned the masterpiece of nature."

86

An Altruistic Spirit

*"Truly, great people live extraordinary lives because,
I believe, for the most part they have an ingrained habit
of always thinking of other people and showing them
kindness."*

— *Norman Vincent Peale*
The Power Of Positive Living

■　■　■

The opposite of egoism is altruism or the unselfish concern for the welfare of others. A hero or heroine is usually caught between the two isms. The very act that helps another person (altruism) can draw an inordinate amount of attention to the hero or heroine and excessive pride (egoism) can result.

On July 22, 1982 while vacationing in Daytona Beach, Florida, I witnessed an act of bravery that was the epitome of altruism. It was a beautiful day by the swimming pool at the Cabana Motel. Suddenly, a young mother screamed at the lifeguard on duty, "Help! It's my little girl," pointing to the bottom of the pool.

The lifeguard, a teenage boy, jumped into the pool and retrieved the little girl. She was limp, blue and unconscious. Then, panic struck. The lifeguard either didn't know what to do or simply forgot in a chaotic moment. The mother begged hysterically, "Somebody PLEASE help my baby!"

Without hesitation, a stocky, mustachioed man rushed to the little girl's side and began to administer CPR. This man knew exactly what to do. He showed extreme professionalism in a life and death situation. After what seemed like an eternity, the little girl responded and was soon breathing normally.

The hero happened to be a man named Johnny, a fireman from Athens, Georgia on his way to a Caribbean cruise. Unfortunately, I never did learn his last name. He was in the right place at the right time. Everyone was applauding and congratulating Johnny on his valiant rescue. He seemed embarrassed by all the fanfare. He said he'd only done what a fireman is trained to do.

On the following day, I saw the little girl, a four-year-old named Michelle Atkins from Rex, Georgia, swimming in the pool under the watchful eye of her mother. It struck me that such a precious young life now had a second chance due to the unselfish, brave effort of a stranger. I knew that fireman wasn't seeking recognition, but I remember writing to Athens Fire Chief Tom Eberhart to explain what happened on that anxious day in Florida.

The moral is quite clear. If we give unselfishly to others, that's enough reward in itself. Nevertheless, I hope Johnny received a nice commendation letter or plaque for his altruistic spirit. Of course, no reward will ever measure up to the satisfaction Johnny must feel in saving Michelle's life. God bless you, Johnny and Michelle, wherever you are.

87

Appreciation

"One of the most neglected virtues of our daily existence is appreciation."

— *Dale Carnegie*
How To Win Friends And Influence People

■ ■ ■

If you'd like to have more money, more success, more love, more happiness or more of anything, simply give more of that which you desire. I believe that maxim is especially true of appreciation.

It's only natural to desire the admiration and acknowledgement of our families, friends and peers. We all like to know when we're doing something well. A few words of encouragement usually go a long way to boosting our self-esteem.

On the other hand, nothing can be more devastating than knowing our efforts are not appreciated; or not knowing if our labors are valued. It's human nature to relish praise. It's quite unnatural to shun recognition. We all want to feel important in our own way.

The secret of getting others more interested in us is getting more interested in others. People aren't nearly as interested in hearing our stories as they are in telling their stores. Learn to listen carefully. Once people know you care about them, they'll gladly become interested in you.

Take the time to compliment others. Do it honestly, sincerely and regularly. Flattery is self-serving, but genuine admiration of the accomplishments of others is good for everyone. A person can go for several weeks on a few kind words of appreciation. Choose your words wisely.

Ask people this magical question, "What do you think?" Those four words are perhaps the greatest way to shower appreciation on others. We all like to think our opinions are valuable. We all like to feel wanted.

Give small tokens of appreciation. A thoughtful thank you note, a bouquet of flowers or a couple of complimentary tickets can be powerful expressions of approval. In truth, most people will be more productive when they understand their commitment is held in high esteem.

Remember, no one succeeds solely on his or her own efforts. If we give consistent credit to the people who help us along the way, we'll probably receive our fair share of appreciation and recognition in due time.

88

A Forgiving Spirit

*"Only the brave know how to forgive . . . a coward
never forgave; it is not in his nature."*
— *Laurence Sterne*

■ ■ ■

Why have a forgiving spirit?

First and foremost, it's Biblical. The Lord's Prayer
commands us to "forgive everyone who sins against us."
(Luke 11:4, NIV) That sounds simple enough in theory, but
the practice of forgiveness can be one of life's most
difficult tasks.

Second, forgiveness is necessary to maintain an orderly
society. Imagine how chaotic the world would be if there
was no forgiveness, if revenge was the chief motivator in
life. Life wouldn't just be stressful, it would be downright
unbearable.

Third, forgiveness is healthy. People who turn a single
incident into a long, deep-seeded bitterness can end up
jeopardizing the mental and physical well-being of all
parties involved. Life is too short to harbor grudges when
a little forgiveness can be such a potent medicine.

A forgiving spirit doesn't mean a person is weak. On the
contrary, it takes a strong, courageous person to cast aside
their ego and say, "I forgive you." Without forgiveness,
consider the alternatives.

Will we lose valuable time and energy needed for other dominant interests in our lives? Will we do something we'll regret for the rest of our lives? Will we let a single incident blind us from all the positive experiences that lie ahead? Will we gain more from our refusal to forgive than what we'd receive if we did forgive?

The difficult part is to forgive AND forget—especially if it's a major disappointment in our lives. Frankly, there are some things we'll never forget and that's okay. The important thing is if we forgive with a sincere heart, we can get on with the rest of our lives even if the memory of a particularly bad incident never disappears.

The greatest reward of forgiveness is freedom. We bear an enormous burden when we refuse to forgive. We lighten our load when we learn to forgive. We experience a glorious freedom of mind, body and spirit. Who knows? In time, we might even forget!

89

A Passion for
Leadership

"Leadership is the art of getting someone else to do something you want done because he wants to do it."
— *Dwight D. Eisenhower*

■ ▪ ■

Thousands of books have been written about leadership and what it takes to be a great leader. Some people can describe these qualities in vivid detail; others just know a great leader when they see one. Of all the blessings a person can have in a lifetime, leadership is one of the most rewarding.

Great leaders are rare because few people are willing to master four special qualities. While there may be many other leadership qualities, these four are crucial:

- *Character*—This quality encompasses integrity, honesty, serving as a worthy role model and exemplifying the purpose of the organization. It's what gives the followers the confidence to trust their leader. Without character, a leader eventually becomes an ex-leader.

- *Common Sense*—The great leaders aren't always the most scholarly people, but they're the most savvy. They think things through. They're decisive. They

---

share their vision with the troops. They surround themselves with experts and aren't afraid to admit they don't know everything.

▸ *Charisma*—This is more than personality. It's character and common sense in action. Above all, it requires superb communication skills—especially speaking skills. General Norman Schwarzkopf, as commander of Operation Desert Storm during the war with Iraq in 1991, was a big hit at the daily television press conferences. It's no coincidence this positive exposure propelled him into a lucrative public speaking career after his military retirement.

▸ *Compassion*—Great leaders realize their success depends upon the success of their people. They care about everyone. They take the time to compliment and to recognize the achievements of their people. They learn to say these four magical words, "I'm proud of you!"

Perhaps no American leader personified these four leadership qualities more than President Abraham Lincoln. "Honest Abe" certainly had character. Lincoln was widely read and highly intelligent, but he had the uncanny ability to simplify things by using old-fashioned common sense. His charisma was best demonstrated by his oratorical skills and, of course, his Gettysburg Address is one of the greatest speeches of all time. Finally, Lincoln displayed uncommon compassion at a time when the United States was being torn apart by the Civil War.

Do you have leadership ability? Use these skills wisely and you'll make everyone around you a better person. In the process, you'll become a better person, too.

90

Health

"The first wealth is health."

— *Ralph Waldo Emerson*

■ ■ ■

We should never take our health for granted. My friend Jim Costello knows the true meaning of that statement. He received a rude wake-up call on February 6, 1989 at the age of 33.

Jim was alone at his office when his jaw began to hurt at 7:10 a.m. By 7:20, he felt nauseated, disoriented and pain in his chest. Fortunately, a fellow employee arrived about that time and drove Jim to nearby St. Joseph's Hospital in Atlanta. By 7:25, Jim's heart had quit beating.

"I died for a few minutes," says Jim. "One artery was 100 percent clogged. I've lost that part of my heart—it's just scar tissue. I remember reading an article in *Reader's Digest* about jaw pain being one of the symptoms of a heart attack."

I was shocked to learn of Jim's heart attack. He was only 33, tall and trim. He exercises regularly, doesn't smoke and maintains a fairly careful diet. What I didn't know was Jim's father, an alcoholic and an angry man, died of a heart attack at 50. Besides carrying the hereditary risk, Jim also carried some of his father's anger, which he feels was a major contributor to his heart attack.

Today, Jim is a changed man. He's learned to control his anger. "My awareness level has increased tenfold," observes Jim. "I believe I've achieved excellence as a father and moved from medium to very good as a husband. When we die, the only thing we have left is our enduring relationships with others."

Jim has made other changes, too. He takes one baby aspirin a day. He's eliminated red meat from his diet. In addition to his vigorous running program, Jim lifts weights and does pushups as a part of his cardiac rehabilitation program. His motivation? "I already died once!"

Seven months after his heart attack—on Labor Day, September 4, 1989—it was an honor to accompany Jim on a 3.1-mile road race. The purpose of the race was to convince members of the International Organizing Committee to bring the 1996 Olympics to Atlanta (one year later, Atlanta was chosen). I have to believe Jim had a different reason for running that morning. I believe it was his way of celebrating good health as a day-to-day gift from God.

91

Hope

"There is no medicine like hope, no incentive so great, and no tonics so powerful as expectation of something better tomorrow."

— *Orison Swett Marden*

■ ■ ■

Hope is what keeps us going. We get out of bed each day hoping to do better than yesterday. If the day isn't so successful, we go to bed hoping for a better tomorrow. It's absolutely amazing how many times the word hope is spoken each day.

Truly, hope is what keeps us enthusiastic about life. In America, we have more reasons to be hopeful than any other nation. Hope is the reason Mexicans risk their lives to cross the Rio Grande into America. It's the reason Haitians brave the perilous Atlantic Ocean in make-shift rafts to reach our shores.

If life is to be lived to its fullest, we can't lose hope for very long. It's the awesome force that propels us into action. It's the wind that breathes new life into us when we've been knocked down. It's the sparkle that gives us the courage to try again on another day.

Without hope, there is no meaningful way to deal with discouragement and defeat. When hope vanishes, life becomes a burden rather than a blessing. Quite often, to lose hope is to give up on life.

Willy Loman, the traveling salesman in Arthur Miller's *Death Of A Salesman*, is a classic example of a dreamer who eventually loses hope. Willy envisions great business and family successes. He's the epitome of optimism and hope. Unfortunately, Willy's sons disappoint him and he's fired from his job at 63. Willy despairs and commits suicide, the worst manifestation of losing hope.

After the funeral, a handful of family members and friends are talking at the cemetery. Biff, Willy's oldest son, says of his father, "He never knew who he was." Charley, Willy's best friend, replies, "A salesman has got to dream, boy. It comes with the territory."

My wish is that your territory will overflow with enthusiastic dreams and limitless hope. Indeed, there is no medicine like hope. As my speaker friend Mike McKinley likes to say, "Wait until you're dead before you die!"

92

Happiness

"You have to believe in happiness,
Or happiness never comes . . .
Ah, that is the reason a bird can sing—
On his darkest day he believes in Spring."
>   — *Douglas Malloch*
>   You Have To Believe

■ ■ ■

Long before Thomas Jefferson penned his famous "pursuit of happiness" phrase in the American Declaration of Independence on July 4, 1776, humankind has been seeking happiness. Unquestionably, happiness can be hard to define, even more difficult to discover.

Actually, I believe happiness is more of an *attitude* than an accomplishment. The Apostle Paul understood this when he said in his letter to the Philippians, ". . . for I have learned to be content whatever the circumstances." (4:11, NIV)

Life has its ups and downs just as surely as the ocean tides roll in and out. If you read Paul's saga in the New Testament, it appears he had a lot more unhappy times than happy ones. Yet, through all his imprisonment, persecution and suffering, Paul "learned to be content." As a result, his writings are the backbone of the Christian religion.

I also believe happiness requires *balance*. Perhaps that's what Channing Pollock meant when he said, "Happiness is a way-station between too little and too much." Workaholics miss out on life's simplest pleasures. Bums fail to contribute their fair share to society. There has to be a balance between work and play.

Jefferson understood all about balance when he said, "It is neither wealth nor splendor, but tranquility and occupation, which gives happiness." To have meaningful life's work and to make time for some tranquil moments amidst the busyness of life is a great recipe for happiness. Like any great recipe, the secret lies in the proper mixture (balance) of ingredients.

Lastly, happiness demands a *clear conscience*. No matter how much we try to impress others in our quest for success, God knows our hearts and we know if our deeds are evil. Consider the wise counsel of Adam Smith: "What can be added to the happiness of a man who is in health, out of debt and has a clear conscience?"

In short, master the ABCs of happiness—attitude, balance and a clear conscience. You'll discover the enjoyment in life you so richly deserve.

93

Tranquility

"Fame and tranquility can never be bedfellows."
— Michel De Montaigne
(1533-1592)

■ ■ ■

Stress can make life seem like a treadmill to nowhere. Is tranquility possible in our search for a meaningful journey to somewhere? Not only is it possible, it's necessary for a reasonably balanced lifestyle.

Doctors often order tranquilizers to relieve people from mental tension. A drug is used to reduce a patient's anxiety without impairing their mental alertness. These patients don't want to be on medication, but their situations warrant such treatment. I'd also like to suggest some other ways to seek tranquility in the spiritual, mental, physical and emotional sides of our lives.

Spiritually, I find unequaled serenity in making time for God through prayer, Bible reading and devotions. Why is it many people have to be on their death beds before they implement these simple but powerful activities? When Lee Atwater, the Republican campaign manager for George Bush in 1988, was dying from a brain tumor, he commented in a *Reader's Digest* article: "For the first time, I read the Bible . . . I sensed a new spiritual presence in my life— something that arrived without my having to call it."

Mentally, I achieve peace of mind by working crossword puzzles, reading and writing. By focusing on these activities, I'm able to relieve the tension I've faced at work or elsewhere. Find your own mental outlets. Make the time to enjoy these stress-relievers.

Physically, I find there is no better way to calm down than aerobic exercise. I look for tranquil spots to run—parks, river trails, scenic neighborhoods. When I travel, I seek out spots with ocean, mountain or historic vistas. If you're not a runner, a brisk walk is quite beneficial and probably just as calming.

Emotionally, I like to have things to look forward to. Judy and I plan our vacations, long weekends and holidays well in advance. From Atlanta, we can be in the Great Smoky Mountains within two-three hours. The serenity of Cades Cove or Gatlinburg in east Tennessee and Maggie Valley or Asheville in western North Carolina is guaranteed to reduce anyone's stress. Find your special havens and visit them as often as possible.

There's enough agitation, disturbance and turmoil in the routine of life. You owe it to yourself (and your family, if applicable) to find some tranquil moments. Enjoy them. Make the most of them. Cherish them.

94

A "No Regrets" Outlook

"Alas, for those who never sing and die with their music still in them."

— *Oliver Wendell Holmes*

■ ■ ■

Within all of us, there exists the potential for greatness. The challenge is in identifying our passion, then doing the best we can to develop our potential. Otherwise, potential is relegated to that abstract abyss known as "what could have been."

It's important to understand there's a big difference between being the best and doing one's best. Striving to be the best is a noble goal, but being No. 1 is usually overrated. It tends to underestimate the value of those who don't finish first. It often deters potential participants from competing due to a fear of failure, namely not being the best.

One of my passions is running. However, I remember being intimidated by the thought of joining the Atlanta Track Club (ATC) and participating in their famous 10,000 kilometer (6.2 miles) road race on July 4—the Peachtree Road Race. I thought the ATC was for world class runners. I feared I'd finish in the back of the pack if I competed in this prestigious event.

Finally, I summoned up the courage to enter my first "Peachtree" in 1978. About 12,000 runners participated and

I finished in a modest, middle-of-the-pack time. Nevertheless, my time was under the 55-minute clock, which qualified me for the coveted Peachtree Road Race T-shirt.

I was so proud of my accomplishment I actually joined the ATC. I've continued to run the "Peachtree" every year since 1978. After the 1981 event, Ron Creasy, Ron Varner and I discussed forming a smaller neighborhood running club. A month later, we officially launched the Chattahoochee Road Runners (CRR).

Since its formation, the CRR has grown to 500 members and is the second largest running club in Georgia behind only the massive ATC. Some of my best friends are "Chattahoochees." Our running club is one of the most respected in the nation. We've donated thousands of dollars to the Leukemia Society from the proceeds of our annual road race.

Belonging to these two running clubs has made me a better person. I've often wondered what I would have missed out on if I'd failed to run my first Peachtree Road Race. Don't deny your passion. Do your best. I'm confident your fondest reward will be an outlook of no regrets.

95

Dignity

"There is a proper dignity and proportion to be observed in the performance of every act of life."
— *Marcus Aurelius Antoninus*
Meditations

■ ■ ■

Everyone deserves to have a sense of dignity, a feeling of worthiness. In our own special way, each of us is important. The challenge is to live up to the dignity we all deserve.

When I think of dignity, I think of my friends Rod and Marilyn Spence. They're soft-spoken, humble people who always seem to have something good to say about everyone. They tend to put the interests of others ahead of their personal concerns.

For example, I remember the first time I ran under 40 minutes in a 10,000 kilometer (6.2 miles) road race in 1982. Although Rod was a much faster runner than I, he paced me all the way. We called him "The Horse" because of his long, loping and seemingly effortless stride. Rod let me cross the finish line first, and that cost him an age group trophy. It didn't phase Rod. He was truly happy to have helped out his friend.

When Judy and I decided to get married in 1984, Rod and Marilyn arranged a gathering of some of our friends at their home. We had a wonderful evening and it remains one of our fondest memories. I don't believe the Spences have an enemy in the world.

Unfortunately, bad things do happen to good people and dignity is put to the test. In 1985, the Spences nearly lost their youngest daughter Kelly in an automobile accident. She made a miraculous recovery from severe head injuries. She's received her master's degree in rehabilitation counseling. Her parents played a major role in her comeback with their encouraging words, positive lifestyle and sense of dignity.

In 1987, tragedy struck Rod. At 47, he was in top physical condition due to competing in marathons and triathlons, and playing at the AA level in tennis. How can anyone explain why a rock happened to be in this man's path while riding his bicycle on a humid evening in Atlanta? He lost control and tumbled into a eight-foot ditch. Fortunately, Rod was with a riding partner or he might have died in that wretched hole.

Rod broke his back and had five vertebrae fused. He's paralyzed from the waist down and is confined to a wheel chair. Has he lost his dignity? Not hardly. He competes in wheel chair road races and tennis tournaments. He drives a specially equipped automobile. He works full-time at an engineering job and has put his three children through college.

Through the good and bad times, the Spences have maintained their dignity. Instead of dwelling on the bad things that have happened to their family, the Spences have risen above these tragic events like the first-class people they are. I call that dignity—a quality truly worth having.

96

Daily Challenge

*"Life that dares send
A challenge to his end,
And when it comes, say,
Welcome, friend!"*

— *Richard Crenshaw*

■ ■ ■

We should be grateful for the challenges of life. Challenge is the substance of optimal living, the difference between existing and excelling.

Remember this about challenge. Don't dwell on the outcome of the challenge. Winning or losing isn't the most important issue. What matters most is *acting* on the daily challenges of life and accepting the consequences provided we gave it our best.

By acting on our challenges, we put ourselves in a win-win situation. How? When we don't measure up to a particular challenge, we can use it as a learning experience. When we conquer a challenge, we enrich our lives and boost our confidence for facing future challenges.

My life is a reflection of this win-win philosophy in dealing with challenge. I didn't respond well to my early high school years and my grades were poor. Fortunately, we moved to Atlanta prior to my sophomore year. Thanks to some special teachers, I responded to the academic challenge and my grades improved dramatically.

When I went off to college, I failed to meet this challenge and dropped out after only one semester. A year later, I joined the Marine Corps and eventually was selected for elite embassy duty in Europe.

After my discharge from the Corps, I went through the motions with several jobs—except for my stint as an Associated Press writer—before choosing to enter the sales profession in 1970. I excelled working on straight commission. In 1982, I accepted a grand challenge by going into business for myself, an opportunity that's provided both discouraging moments and prosperous times.

I married in 1970 and it ended in divorce nearly three years later. I was single for 11 years before marrying Judy in 1984. I learned from the failure of my first marriage and now have what I'd consider a highly successful (but not perfect) marriage.

The pattern is obvious. I've experienced failure and success with the many challenges of my life, but I've refused to let the outcomes deter my willingness to act. Thank God for life's daily challenges. Accept them. Act upon them. Acquire experience from them.

97

Meaningful Life's Work

"Every man's work . . . is always a portrait of himself, and the more he tries to conceal himself the more clearly will his character appear in spite of him."
— *Samuel J. Butler*
The Way Of All Flesh

■ ■ ■

If a person truly loves their life's work, how can it be work? Since most of us will spend a good portion of our lives on the job, we might as well find one we love to do.

Let's face it. There is no perfect career. Even as an entrepreneur, I have the financial risk and the constant challenge of finding new business. I have to make a lot of lonely decisions. If something goes wrong, I'm responsible. So what's the secret of career contentment?

I firmly believe every person possesses innate aptitudes. Call it a natural ability to learn or special talents. I took an aptitude test in my senior year of high school and scored highest in writing, speaking, persuasive and clerical skills. My career has followed that path with amazing accuracy.

In the Marine Corps, I was an administrative clerk prior to becoming an embassy guard. I was a writer for *The Atlanta Constitution* and Associated Press. I've been in the sales profession since 1970, a business owner since 1982 and a professional speaker and trainer since 1986. Even though the jobs have changed in my career, I've always remained true to the skills I love the most.

Alas, the "secret" of career fulfillment isn't really a secret at all. I believe it's contained in the title of Marsha Sinetar's marvelous book, *Do What You Love, The Money Will Follow*. While I'm convinced anyone who says money isn't important will also lie about other things, working at what you love to do is more fulfilling than any amount of financial compensation.

In fact, Dr. Erdman Palmore told me Duke University's First Longitudinal Study Of Aging followed 233 persons age 60 or older for 25 years (1955-80). "Work satisfaction was the strongest single predictor contributing to human longevity for men age 60-69," said Dr. Palmore, "and was the No. 2 contributor for men age 70+." While work satisfaction was less important for women, Dr. Palmore pointed out "work was not necessarily employment" for many women during the early years of this study. Undoubtedly, women of the 1980s and 1990s will find employment satisfaction to be a more important contributor to human longevity.

But beware! A loveable career can be paradoxical. Work—perhaps more than anything else in life—can become an addiction, an obsession. A workaholic can destroy any semblance of balance in life while wrecking a lot of relationships along the way. No career can take the place of meaningful relationships with family and friends. No amount of professional success is worthwhile if personal happiness is forfeited.

Some 2,500 years ago, Theognis said "moderation is best in all things." It's possible to do anything to excess. Only each individual can determine what constitutes excessiveness. Love your work by the wise use of your God-given talents. Love life by making time for all the other wonders God has provided.

98

Financial Convenience

"Money is never an end in itself, but is merely a resource used to accomplish other goals and obligations."

— *Ron Blue, CPA*
Master Your Money

■ ■ ■

Do we work for money or do we work to have the convenience money provides? I believe the answer is convenience. Otherwise, we'd simply save our money, sleep outdoors, subsist off the land and make all of our clothing.

Indeed, money buys convenience. It's simply a matter of how much money a person has and how much convenience is desired. All we really need to survive is adequate food, clothing and shelter. Beyond these essentials, everything else is a convenience.

The question now becomes, "How much money do I need versus how much do I want?" Once we go beyond needs to wants, we're moving from the basics to the conveniences. How we handle this transition is crucial in identifying us as creed-oriented or greed-driven people.

Creed-oriented people understand why no amount of money is ever enough. Oh, they appreciate the nice things money can buy. However, they also know if they lost everything, they'd still have the solid core values and beliefs that enabled them to earn a respectable living in the first place.

Greed-driven people always want more money so they can acquire more things. They do whatever it takes—illegally, unethically or whatever—to succeed financially. Wealth becomes an obsession, a raison d'etre. As long as there's more money and more things, all seems well. Yet, the greed that drives such an obsession is the very poison that usually destroys these people.

Unfortunately, greed is like a cancer. Often, everything seems fine for years as great wealth is accumulated. On the outside, there are many signs of success. On the inside, the cancer (greed) is growing slowly but surely. If the cancer is diagnosed early, it's possible to eliminate the problem. If the cancer is diagnosed too late, it's often fatal and no amount of wealth can stop it.

Money—and the convenience money buys—will never provide long-term fulfillment when greed is the driving force. The quest for true riches is not to be found in the unsatiable thirst for more and more possessions because enough is never enough. Rather, the secret is learning to be content with whatever conveniences we are blessed with and to realize true riches are found in people and profound purposes, not possessions and petty greed.

99

True Success

"Is success, true success, worth the struggle?"
— *Og Mandino*
University Of Success

■ ■ ■

What is true success? The very question implies there's a difference between success and *true* success. I believe there is.

Generally, success is measured materially by luxurious homes, expensive automobiles, big boats, fancy offices, money and other property. While all of these things are nice, are they really a measure of true success? Will any of these "toys" go with us in death?

I believe the problem with achieving professional (or material) success is one of emptiness. Psychologist Dr. Douglas LaBier, author of *Modern Madness: The Emotional Fallout Of Success*, confirmed such emptiness in one of his research projects. More than half the successful people LaBier interviewed told him they "like the perks (of success), but they say their life is too thin, too boring, and that they don't know what to do about it."

True success, on the other hand, isn't measured professionally or materially. Best of all, the rewards are lasting and fulfilling. I believe there are at least three marks of true success:

---

*,—The major difference between success and ..c success is integrity. A person with integrity enjoys a reputation built upon soundness of character. Dwight Moody said, "Character is what a person has in the dark."

► *Impact On Others*—A person with integrity sets an example for others as a good role model. The word impact means to make "a powerful impression" and, hopefully, a positive one on the people around you. Are you making a favorable difference in the lives of other people? If so, congratulations and keep it up! If not, why not?

► *Immortality With God*—Your religious faith (or lack of it) is a personal matter. However, the word immortality or "unending existence" excites me. We're talking about eternal life with God in heaven. That's a lot more enduring than any riches, fame or power we'll accumulate here on earth.

So, is true success worth the struggle? I'm convinced it is, provided a person can answer an honest yes to these questions:

1. Did I strive to maintain my *integrity*?
2. Did I have a positive *impact* on others?
3. Will I have *immortality* with God in heaven?

100

Maturity

"It takes a long time to bring excellence to maturity."
— *Publilius Syrus*
(Circa 42 B.C.)

■ ■ ■

We should always be in a state of maturation. Maturity blends the enthusiasm of youth with the experience of adulthood to form a better human being.

Maturity, by its very nature, is about *time*. Just as fine wine requires aging, people need seasoning. The challenge lies in being patient until our talents have sufficient time to develop. Fortunately, the process is worth the wait.

In addition, maturity requires *tolerance*. We have to adapt to many unfamiliar environments while we're polishing our life's skills. The process is personal growth. Meantime, we must tolerate a lot of humbling learning experiences as we progress towards a state of maturity.

Furthermore, maturity requires *tenacity*. It takes an intrepid spirit to press on in spite of mistakes, setbacks and failures. However, the ability to overcome adversity is a major part of maturity. As we develop, it becomes clear that tenacity is a vital quality in achieving any worthwhile goal.

Perhaps more than anything, maturity requires *truthfulness*. We have to recognize our strengths and make the most of them. More importantly, we shouldn't deceive ourselves by making excuses for our weaknesses or we become masters of rationalization. The key to maturity is developing our weaknesses into strengths without being untrue to ourselves during the process.

This "To Have" section is a reflection of the bountiful blessings that can be ours when we understand the proper alignment of the four forces of balanced living advocated in this book. Emotionally, we feel better about ourselves because we have learned to put our faith in God Almighty instead of the almighty dollar; and to value our relationships more than selfishness. In short, we understand the difference between . . .

Immaturity: Have → Think → Do → Be = Unbalanced Lifestyle

Maturity: Be → Think → Do → Have = Balanced Lifestyle

Epilogue

"ONLY through living a balanced life will you ever reach the point of being successful . . . and happy!"
— *Gene Swindell*
The ABC's Of Success

■ ■ ■

Whew! By now, you're probably thinking no one is capable of implementing all these suggestions for more balanced living. I agree.

Perfection should not be your goal. The objective should be a willingness to gradually improve your lifestyle by becoming more balanced. As you gain wisdom, experience and maturity, I hope you'll believe in the value of a balanced lifestyle based on a philosophy of genuine goodness.

I couldn't have written this book at age 20, 30 or 40 because I was still green and growing. While I'm a long way from being as ripe as I'd like to be, I'm striving to cultivate a bumper crop. Such a cultivation process includes fertile soil, fresh air, adequate water and plenty of sunshine. Just as soil, air, water and sunshine in union create the balance required to produce a bountiful harvest, it's also necessary to blend the spiritual, mental, physical and emotional forces into the cultivation of a balanced lifestyle.

Remember, balanced living is possible when viewed as a process, pursued persistently and practiced patiently over a period of years. Are you prepared to participate in this process? If so, I promise you prosperity and pleasure beyond your most profound imagination.

About the Author

Dick Biggs is president of Biggs Automobile Leasing Corp. in Roswell, Georgia.

In addition to his leasing activities, Dick conducts automobile leasing seminars for a host of manufacturers, dealerships, financial institutions and automobile associations. He was the first Certified Vehicle Leasing Executive (CVLE) in Georgia and is one of only 150 in the nation. Also, he is a past recipient of the Clemens-Pender Award, the highest recognition granted in the vehicle leasing industry.

Dick is in demand as an inspirational speaker and balanced living seminar leader. He's a member of the National Speakers Association and a past president of the Georgia Speakers Association.

He is active in his church as a Sunday school teacher. He and his wife reside in Roswell, some 25 miles north of Atlanta.

Give the Gift of Balanced Living to Your Friends and Colleagues

ORDER FORM

YES, I want ___ copies of *If Life Is A Balancing Act, Why Am I So Darn Clumsy?* at $22.95 each, plus $3 shipping per book (Georgia residents please add $1.38 state sales tax per book). Canadian orders must be accompanied by a postal money order in U.S. funds. Allow 15 days for delivery.

☐ **YES**, I am interested in having Dick Biggs speak or give a seminar on balanced living to my company, association, school, or organization. Please send information.

My check or money order for $_____ is enclosed.
Please charge my ☐ Visa ☐ MasterCard

Name _____ Phone _____

Organization _____

Address _____

City/State/Zip _____

Card # _____ Exp. Date _____

Signature _____

Please make your check payable and return to:
Chattahoochee Publishers
420 Market Place, Suite 108
Roswell, Georgia 30075

Or call/fax your credit card order to:
Phone: (404) 998-5452
Fax: (404) 998-5513